Reflections and Comments 1865-1895

Edwin Lawrence Godkin

Contents

PEACE 7
CULTURE AND WAR 12
THE COMPARATIVE MORALITY OF NATIONS 16
THE "COMIC-PAPER" QUESTION.. 21
MR. FROUDE AS A LECTURER... 26
MR. HORACE GREELEY.. 30
THE MORALS AND MANNERS OF THE KITCHEN 34
JOHN STUART MILL.. 40
PANICS... 46
THE ODIUM PHILOLOGICUM 54
PROFESSOR HUXLEY'S LECTURES.. 58
CIRCUMSTANTIAL EVIDENCE 65
TYNDALL AND THE THEOLOGIANS 71
THE CHURCH AND SCIENCE 75
THE CHURCH AND GOOD CONDUCT 79
ROLE OF THE UNIVERSITIES IN POLITICS 83
THE HOPKINS UNIVERSITY 87
THE SOUTH AFTER THE WAR... 92
   I 92
   II 97
CHROMO-CIVILIZATION 101
"THE SHORT-HAIRS" AND.. 108
"THE SWALLOW-TAILS"... 108
JUDGES AND WITNESSES 114
"THE DEBTOR CLASS".. 118
COMMENCEMENT ADMONITION 122
"ORGANS".. 125
EVIDENCE ABOUT CHARACTER 128
PHYSICAL FORCE IN POLITICS 131
"COURT CIRCLES" 136
LIVING IN EUROPE AND GOING TO IT 140
CARLYLE'S POLITICAL INFLUENCE 146
THE EVOLUTION OF THE SUMMER RESORT 150
SUMMER REST 157
THE SURVIVAL OF TYPES 160
WILL WIMBLES.. 163

REFLECTIONS AND COMMENTS 1865-1895

BY

Edwin Lawrence Godkin

TO CHARLES ELIOT NORTON TO WHOM THE FOUNDATION OF "THE NATION" WAS LARGELY DUE, IN GRATEFUL ACKNOWLEDG-MENT OF A LONG FRIENDSHIP

REFLECTIONS AND COMMENTS
1865-1895

PEACE

The horrors of war are just now making a deeper impression than ever on the popular mind, owing to the close contact with the battle-field and the hospital into which the railroad and the telegraph and the newspaper have brought the public of all civilized countries. Wars are fought out now, so to speak, under every man's and woman's eyes; and, what is perhaps of nearly as much importance, the growth of commerce and manufactures, and the increased complication of the social machine, render the smallest derangement of it any-where a concern and trouble to all nations. The consequence is that the desire for peace was never so deep as it is now, and the eagerness of all good people to find out some other means of deciding international disputes than mutual killing never so intense.

And yet the unconsciousness of the true nature and difficulties of the problem they are trying to solve, which is displayed by most of those who make the advo-cacy of peace their special work, is very discouraging. We are far from believing that the incessant and direct appeals to the public conscience on the subject of war are not likely in the long run to produce some effect; but it is very difficult to resist the conclusion that the efforts of the special advocates of peace have thus far helped to spread and strengthen the impression that there is no adequate substitute for the sword as an arbiter between nations, or, in other words, to harden the popular heart on the subject of military slaughter. It is certain that, during the last fifty years, the period in which peace societies have been at work, armies have been growing steadily larger, the means of destruction have been multiplying, and wars have been as frequent and as bloody as ever before; and, what is worse, the popular heart goes into war as it has never done in past ages.

The great reason why the more earnest enemies of war have not made more progress toward doing away with it, has been that, from the very outset of their labors down to the present moment, they have devoted themselves mainly to depicting its horrors and to denouncing its cruelty. In other words, they almost invariably approach it from a side with which nations actually engaged in it are just as familiar as anybody, but which has for the moment assumed in their eyes a secondary importance. The peace advocates are constantly talking of the guilt of killing, while the combatants only think, and will only think, of the nobleness of dying. To the peace advocates the soldier is always a man going to slaughter his neighbors; to his countrymen he is a man going to lose his life for their sake--that is, to perform the loftiest act of devotion of which a human being is capable. It is not wonderful, then, that the usual effect of appeals for peace made by neutrals is to produce mingled exasperation and amusement among the belligerents. To the great majority of Europeans our civil war was a shocking spectacle, and the persistence of the North in carrying it on a sad proof of ferocity and lust of dominion. To the great majority of those engaged in carrying it on the struggle was a holy one, in which it was a blessing to perish. Probably nothing ever fell more cruelly on human ears than the taunts and execrations which American wives and mothers heard from the other side of the ocean, heaped on the husbands and sons whom they had sent to the battle-field, never thinking at all of their slaying, but thinking solely of their being slain; and very glad indeed that, if death had to come, it should come in such a cause. If we go either to France or Germany to-day, we shall find a precisely similar state of feeling. If the accounts we hear be true--and we know of no reason to doubt them--there is no more question in the German and French mind that French and German soldiers are doing their highest duty in fighting, than there was in the most patriotic Northern or Southern home during our war; and we may guess, therefore, how a German or French mother, the light of whose life had gone out at Gravelotte or Orleans, and who hugs her sorrow as a great gift of God, would receive an address from New York on the general wickedness and folly of her sacrifice.

The fact is--and it is one of the most suggestive facts we know of--that the very growth of the public conscience has helped to make peace somewhat more difficult, war vastly more terrible. When war was the game of kings and soldiers, the nations went into it in a half-hearted way, and sincerely loathed it; now that war is literally an outburst of popular feeling, the friend of peace finds most of his logic powerless. There is little use in reasoning with a man who is ready to die on the folly or wickedness of dying. When a nation has worked itself up to the point of believing that there are objects within its reach for which life were well surrendered, it has reached a region in which the wise saws and modern instances of the philosopher or lawyer cannot touch it, and in which pictures of the misery of war only help to make the martyr's crown seem more glorious.

Therefore, we doubt whether the work of peace is well done by those who, amidst the heat and fury of actual hostilities, dwell upon the folly and cruelty of them, and appeal to the combatants to stop fighting, on the ground that fighting involves suffering and loss of life, and the destruction of property. The principal effect of this on "the average man" has been to produce the impression that the friends of peace are ninnies, and to make him smile over the earnestness with which everybody looks on his own wars as holy and inevitable, and his neighbors' wars as unnecessary and wicked. Any practical movement to put an end to war must begin far away from the battle-field and its horrors. It must take up and deal with the various influences, social and political, which create and perpetuate the state of mind which makes people ready to fight. Preaching up peace and preaching down war generally are very like general homilies in praise of virtue and denunciation of vice. Everybody agrees with them, but nobody is ever ready to admit their applicability to his particular case. War is, in our time, essentially the people's work. Its guilt is theirs, as its losses and sufferings are theirs. All attempts to saddle emperors, kings, and nobles with the responsibility of it may as well be given up from this time forward.

Now, what are the agencies which operate in producing the frame of mind which makes people ready to go to war on small provocation? It is at these the friends of peace must strike, in time of peace, and not after the cannon has begun to roar and the country has gone mad with patriotism and rage. They are, first of all, the preaching in the press and elsewhere of the false and pernicious doctrine that one nation gains by another's losses, and can be made happy by its misery; that the United States, for instance, profits in the long run by the prostration of French, German, or English industry. One of the first duties of a peace society is to watch this doctrine, and hunt it down wherever they see it, as one of the great promoters of the pride and hardness of heart which make war seem a trifling evil. America can no more gain by French or German ruin than New York can gain by that of Massachusetts. Secondly, there is the mediaeval doctrine that the less commercial intercourse nations carry on with each other the better for both, and that markets won or kept by force are means of gain. There has probably been no more fruitful source of war than this. It has for three centuries desolated the world, and all peace associations should fix on it, wherever they encounter it, the mark of the beast. Thirdly, there is the tendency of the press, which is now the great moulder of public opinion, to take what we may call the pugilist's view of international controversies. The habit of taunting foreign disputants, sneering at the cowardice or weakness of the one who shows any sign of reluctance in drawing the sword, and counting up the possible profit to its own country of one or other being well thrashed, in which it so frequently indulges, has inevitably the effect not only of goading the disputants into hostilities, but of connecting in the popular mind at home the idea of unreadiness or unwillingness to fight with baseness and meanness and material disadvantage. Fourthly, there is the practice, to which the press, orators, and poets in every civilized country steadily adhere, of maintaining, as far as their influence goes, the same notions about national honor which once prevailed about individual "honor"--that is, the notion that it is discreditable to acknowledge one's self in the wrong, and always more becoming to fight than apologize. "The code" has been abandoned in the Northern States and in England in the regulations of the relations of individual men, and a duellist is looked on, if not as a wicked, as a crack-brained person; but in some degree in both of them, and in a great degree in all other countries, it still regulates the mode in which international quarrels are brought to a conclusion.

Last of all, and most important of all, it is the duty of peace societies to cherish and exalt the idea of *law* as the only true controller of international relations, and discourage and denounce their submission to **sentiment**. The history of civilization is the history of the growth amongst human beings of the habit of submitting their dealings with each other to the direction of rules of universal application, and their withdrawal of them from the domain of personal feeling. The history of "international law" is the history of the efforts of a number of rulers and statesmen to induce nations to submit themselves to a similar regime--that is, to substitute precedents and rules based on general canons of morality and on principles of municipal law, for the dictates of pride, prejudice, and passion, in their mode of seeking redress of injuries, of interpreting contracts, exchanging services, and carrying on commercial dealings. Their success thus far has been only partial. A nation, even the most highly civilized, is still, in its relations with its fellows, in a condition somewhat analogous to that of the individual savage. It chooses its friends from whim or fancy, makes enemies through ignorance or caprice, avenges its wrongs in a torrent of rage, or through a cold-blooded thirst for plunder, and respects rules and usages only fitfully, and with small attention to the possible effect of its disregard of them on the general welfare. The man or the woman and, let us say, "the mother"--since that is supposed to be, in this discussion, a term of peculiar potency--who tries to exert a good influence on public opinion on all these points, to teach the brotherhood of man as an economical as well as a moral and religious truth; to spread the belief that war between any two nations is a general calamity to the civilized world; that it is as unchristian and inhuman to rouse national combativeness as to rouse individual combativeness, as absurd to associate honor with national wrong-doing as with individual wrong-doing; and that peace among nations, as among individuals, is, and can only be, the product of general reverence for **law** and general distrust of **feeling**--may rest assured that he or she is doing far more to bring war to an end than can be done by the most fervid accounts of the physical suffering it causes. It will be a sorrowful day for any people when their men come to consider death on the battle-field the greatest of evils, and the human heart will certainly have sadly fallen off when those who stay at home have neither gratitude nor admiration for those who shoulder the musket, or are impressed less by the consideration that the soldiers are going to kill others than by the consideration that they are going to die themselves. There are things worth cherishing even in war; and the seeds of what is worst in it are sown not in camps, barracks, or forts, but in public meetings and newspapers and legislatures and in literature.

CULTURE AND WAR

The feeling of amazement with which the world is looking on at the Prussian campaigns comes not so much from the tremendous display of physical force they afford--though there is in this something almost appalling--as from the consciousness which everybody begins to have that to put such an engine of destruction as the German army into operation there must be behind it a new kind of motive power. It is easy enough for any government to put its whole male population under arms, or even to lead them on an emergency to the field. But that an army composed in the main of men suddenly taken from civil pursuits should fight and march, as the Prussian army is doing, with more than the efficiency of any veteran troops the world has yet seen, and that the administrative machinery by which they are fed, armed, transported, doctored, shrived, and buried should go like clock-work on the enemy's soil, and that the people should submit not only without a murmur, but with enthusiasm, to sacrifices such as have never before been exacted of any nation except in the very throes of despair, show that something far more serious has taken place in Prussia than the transformation of the country into a camp. In other words, we are not witnessing simply a levy *en masse*, nor yet the mere maintenance of an immense force by a military monarchy, but the application to military affairs of the whole intelligence of a nation of great mental and moral culture. The peculiarity of the Prussian system does not lie in the size of its armies or the perfection of its armament, but in the character of the men who compose it. All modern armies, except Cromwell's "New Model Army" and that of the United States during the rebellion, have been composed almost entirely of ignorant peasants drilled into passive obedience to a small body of professional soldiers. The Prussian army is the first, however, to be a perfect reproduction of the society which sends it to the field. To form it, all Prussian men lay down their tools or pens or books, and shoulder muskets. Consequently, its excellences and defects are those of the community at large, and the community at large being cultivated in a remarkable degree, we get for the first time in history a real example of the devotion of mind and training, on a great scale, to the work of destruction.

Of course, the quality of the private soldier has in all wars a good deal to do with making or marring the fortunes of commanders; but it is safe to say that no strategists have over owed so much to the quality of their men as the Prussian strategists. Their perfect handling of the great masses which are now manoeuvring in France has been made in large degree possible by the intelligence of the privates. This has been strikingly shown on two or three occasions by the facility with which whole regiments or brigades have been sacrificed in carrying a single position. With ordinary troops, only a certain amount can be deliberately and openly exacted of any one corps. The highest heights of devotion are often beyond their reach. But if it serves the purposes of a Prussian commander to have all the cost of an assault fall on one regiment, he apparently finds not the slightest difficulty in getting it to march to certain destruction, and not blindly as peasants march, but as men of education, who understand the whole thing, but having made it for this occasion their business to die, do it like any other duty of life--not hilariously or enthusiastically or recklessly, but calmly and energetically, as they study or manufacture or plough. They get themselves killed not one particle more than is necessary, but also not one particle less.

A nation organized in this way is a new phenomenon, and is worth attentive study. It gives one a glimpse of possibilities in the future of modern civilization of which few people have hitherto dreamed, and it must be confessed that the prospect is not altogether pleasing. We have been flattering ourselves--in Anglo-Saxondom, at least--for many years back that all social progress was to be hereafter in the direction of greater individualism, and among us, certainly, this view has derived abundant support from observed facts. But it is now apparent that there is a tendency at work, which appears to grow stronger and stronger every day, toward combination in all the work of life. It is specially observable in the efforts of the working classes to better their condition; it still more observable in the efforts of capital to fortify itself against them and against the public at large; and there is, perhaps, nothing in which more rapid advances have been made of late years than in the power of organization. The working of the great railroads and hotels and manufactories, of the trades unions, of the co-operative associations, and of the monster armies now maintained by three or four powers, are all illustrations of it. The growth of power is, of course, the result of the growth of intelligence, and it is in the ratio of the growth of intelligence.

Prussia has got the start of all other countries by combining the whole nation in one vast organization for purposes of offence and defence. Hitherto nations have simply subscribed toward the maintenance of armies and concerned themselves little about their internal economy and administration; but the Prussians have converted themselves into an army, and have been enabled to do so solely by subjecting themselves to a long process of elaborate training, which has changed the national character. When reduced to the lowest point of humiliation after the battle of Jena, they went to work and absolutely built up the nation afresh. We may not altogether like the result. To large numbers of people the Prussian type of character is not a pleasing one, nor Prussian society an object of unmixed admiration, and there is something horrible in a whole people's passing their best years learning how to kill. But we cannot get over the fact that the Prussian man is likely to furnish, consciously or unconsciously, the model to other civilized countries, until such time as some other nation has so successfully imitated him as to produce his like.

Let those who believe, as Mr. Wendell Phillips says that he believes, that "the best education a man can get is what he gets in picking up a living," and that universities are humbugs, and that from the newspapers and lyceum lecture the citizen can always get as much information on all subjects, human and divine, as is good for him or the State, take a look at the Prussian soldier as he marches past in his ill-fitting uniform and his leather helmet. First of all, we observe that he smokes a great deal. According to some of us, the "tobacco demon" ought by this time to have left him a thin, puny, hollow-eyed fellow, with trembling knees and palpitating heart and listless gait, with shaking hands and an intense craving for ardent spirits. You perceive, however, that a burlier, broader-shouldered, ruddier, brighter-eyed, and heartier-looking man you never set eyes on; and as he swings along in column, with his rifle, knapsack, seventy rounds of ammunition, blanket, and saucepan, you must confess you cannot help acknowledging that you feel sorry for any equal body of men in the world with which that column may get into "a difficulty." He drinks, too, and drinks a great deal, both of strong beer and strong wine, and has always done so, and all his family friends do it, and have only heard of teetotalism through the newspapers, and, if you asked him to confine himself to water, would look on you as an amiable idiot. Nevertheless, you never see him drunk, nor does his beer produce on him that utterly bemuddling or brain-paralyzing effect which is so powerfully described by our friend Mr. James Parton as produced on him by lager-bier, in that inquiry into the position of "The Coming Man" toward wine, some copies of which, we see, he is trying to distribute among the field-officers. On the contrary, he is, on the whole, a very sober man, and very powerful thinker, and very remarkable scholar. There is no field of human knowledge which he has not been among the first to explore; no heights of speculation which he has not scaled; no problem of the world over which he is not fruitfully toiling. Moreover, his thoroughness is the envy of the students of all other countries, and his hatred of sham scholarship and slipshod generalization is intense.

But what with the tobacco and the beer, and the scholarship and his university education, you might naturally infer that he must be a kid-glove soldier, and a little too nice and dreamy and speculative for the actual work of life. But you never were more mistaken. He is leaving behind him some of the finest manufactories and best-tilled fields in the world. Moreover, he is an admirable painter and, as all the world knows, an almost unequalled musician; or if you want proof of his genius for business, look at the speed and regularity with which he and his comrades have transported themselves to the Rhine, and see the perfection of all the arrangements of his regiment. And now, if you think his "bad habits," his daily violations of your notions of propriety, have diminished his power of meeting death calmly--that noblest of products of culture--you have only to follow him up as far as Sedan and see whether he ever flinches; whether you have ever read or heard of a soldier out of whom more marching and fighting and dying, and not flighty, boisterous dying either, could be got.

Now, we can very well understand why people should be unwilling to see the Prussian military system spread into other countries, or even be preserved where it is. It is a pitiful thing to have the men of a whole civilized nation spending so much time out of the flower of their years learning to kill other men; and the lesson to be drawn from the recent Prussian successes is assuredly not that every country ought to have an army like the Prussian army, though we confess that, if great armies must be kept up, there is no better model than the Prussian. The lesson is that, whether you want him for war or peace, there is no way in which you can get so much out of a man as by training him, and training him not in pieces but the whole of him; and that the trained men, other things being equal, are pretty sure in the long run to be the masters of the world.

THE COMPARATIVE MORALITY OF NATIONS

We had, four or five weeks ago, a few words of controversy with the **Christian Union** as to the comparative morality of the Prussians and Americans, or, rather, their comparative religiousness--meaning by religiousness a disposition "to serve others and live as in God's sight;" in other words, unselfishness and spirituality. We let it drop, from the feeling that the question whether the Americans or Prussians were the better men was only a part, and a very small part, of the larger question. How do we discover which of any two nations is the purer in its life or in its aims? and, is not any judgment we form about it likely to be very defective, owing to the inevitable incompleteness of our premises? We are not now going to try to fix the place of either Prussia or the United States in the scale of morality, but to point out some reasons why all comparisons between them should be made by Americans with exceeding care and humility. There is hardly any field of inquiry in which even the best-informed man is likely to fall into so many errors; first, because there is no field in which the vision is so much affected by prejudices of education and custom; and, secondly, because there is none in which the things we see are so likely to create erroneous impressions about the things we do not see. But we may add that it is a field which no intelligent and sensible man ever explores without finding his charity greatly stimulated.

Let us give some illustrations of the errors into which people are apt to fall in it. Count Gasparin, a French Protestant, and as spiritually minded a man as breathed, once talking with an American friend expressed in strong terms his sense of the pain it caused him that Mr. Lincoln should have been at the theatre when he was killed, not, the friend found, because he objected in the least to theatre-going, but because it was the evening of Good Friday--a day which the Continental Calvinists "keep" with great solemnity, but to which American non-episcopal Protestants pay no attention whatever. Count Gasparin, on the other hand, would have no hesitation in taking a ride on Sunday, or going to a public promenade after church hours, and, from seeing him there, his American friend would draw deductions just as unfavorable to the Count's religious character as the Count himself drew with regard to Mr. Lincoln's.

Take, again, the question of drinking beer and wine. There is a large body of very excellent men in America who, from a long contemplation of the evils wrought by excessive indulgence in intoxicating drinks, have worked themselves up to a state of mind about all use of such drinks which is really discreditable to reasonable beings, leads to the most serious platform excesses, and is perfectly incomprehensible to Continental Europeans. To the former, the drinking even of lager beer connotes, as the logicians say, ever so many other vices--grossness and sensuality of nature, extravagance, indifference to home pleasures, repugnance to steady industry, and a disregard of the precepts of religion and morality. To many of them a German workman, and his wife and children, sitting in a beer-garden on a summer's evening, which to European moralists and economists is one of the most pleasing sights in the world, is a revolting spectacle, which calls for the interference of the police. Now, if you go to a beer-garden in Berlin you may, any Sunday afternoon, see doctors of divinity--none of your rationalists--but doctors of real divinity, to whom American theologians go to be taught, doing this very thing, and, what is worse, smoking pipes. An American who applied to this the same course of reasoning which he would apply to a similar scene in America, would simply be guilty of outrageous folly. If he argued from it that the German doctor was selfish, or did not "live as in the sight of God," the whole process would be a model of absurdity.

Foreigners have drawn, on the other hand, from the American "diligence in business," conclusions with regard to American character far more uncomplimentary than those the **Christian Union** has expressed with regard to the Prussians. There are not a few religious and moral and cultivated circles in Europe in which the suggestion that Americans, as a nation, were characterized by thoughtfulness for others and a sense of God's presence would be received with derisive laughter, owing to the application to the phenomena of American society of the process of reasoning on which, we fear, the **Union** relies. Down to the war, so candid and perspicacious a man as John Stuart Mill might have been included in this class. The earlier editions of his "Elements of Political Economy" contained a contemptuous statement that one sex in America was entirely given up to "dollar-hunting" and the other to "breeding dollar-hunters." In other words, he held that the American people were plunged in the grossest materialism, and he doubtless based this opinion on that intense application of the men to commercial and industrial pursuits which we see all around us, which no church finds fault with, but which, we know, bad as its effects are on art and literature, really coexists with great generosity, sympathy, public spirit, and ideality.

Take, again, the matter of chastity, on which the *Union* touched. We grant at the outset that wherever you have classes, the women of the lower class suffer more or less from the men of the upper class, and anybody who says that seductions, accomplished through the effect on female vanity of the addresses of "superiors in station," while almost unknown here, are very numerous in Europe, would find plenty of facts to support him. But, on the other hand, an attempt made to persuade a Frenchman that the familiar intercourse which the young people of both sexes in this country enjoy was generally pure, would fail in ninety-nine cases out of a hundred. That it should be pure is opposed to all his experience of human nature, both male and female; and the result of your argument with him would be that he would conclude either that you were an extraordinarily simple person, or took him for one.

On the other hand, we believe the German, who thinks nothing of drinking as much wine or beer as he cares for, draws from the conduct of the American young woman whom he sees abroad, and from what he reads in our papers about "free love," Indiana divorces, abortion, and what not, conclusions with regard to American chastity very different from those of the *Union*; and, if you sought to meet him in discussion, he would overwhelm you with facts and cases which, looked at apart from the general tenor of American life and manners, it would be very hard to dispose of. He would say, for instance, that we are not, perhaps, guilty of as many violations of the marriage vows as Europeans; but that we make it so light a vow that, instead of violating it, we get it abrogated, and then follow our will; and then he would come down on us with boarding-house and hotel life, and other things of the same kind, which might make us despise him, but would make it a little difficult to get rid of him.

There is probably no minor point of manners which does more to create unfavorable impressions of Europeans among the best class of Americans--morally the best, we mean--than the importance attached by the former to their eating and drinking; while there is nothing which does more to spread in Europe impressions unfavorable to American civilization than the indifference of Americans, and, we may add, as regards the progressive portion of American society--cultivated indifference--to the quality of their meals and the time of eating them. In no European country is moderate enjoyment of the pleasures of the table considered incompatible with high moral aims, or even a sincerely religious character; but a man to whom his dinner was of serious importance would find his position in an assembly of American reformers very precarious. The German or Frenchman or Englishman, indeed, treats a man's views of food, and his disposition or indisposition to eat it in company with his fellows as an indication of his place in civilization. Savages love to eat alone, and it has been observed in partially civilized communities relapsing into barbarism, that one of the first indications of their decline was the abandonment of regular meals on tables, and a tendency on the part of the individuals to retire to secret places with their victuals. This is probably a remnant of the old aboriginal instinct which we still see in domesticated dogs, and was, doubtless, implanted for the protection of the species in times when everybody looked on his neighbor's bone with a hungry eye, and the man with the strong hand was apt to have the fullest stomach. Accordingly, there is in Europe, and indeed everywhere, a tendency to regard the growth of a delicacy in eating, and close attention to the time and manner of serving meals and their cookery, and the use of them as promoters of social intercourse, as an indication of moral as well as material progress. To a large number of people here, on the other hand, the bolting of food--ten-minute dinners, for instance--and general unconsciousness of "what is on the table," is a sign of preoccupation with serious things. It may be; but the German love of food is not necessarily a sign of grossness, and that "overfed" appearance, of which the **Union** spoke, is not necessarily a sign of inefficiency, any more than leanness or cadaverousness is a sign of efficiency. There is certainly some power of hard work in King William's army, and, indeed, we could hardly point to a better illustration of the truth, that all the affairs of men, whether political, social, or religious, depend for their condition largely on the state of the digestion.

Honesty, by which we mean that class of virtues which Cicero includes in the term *bona fides*, has, to a considerable extent, owing, we think, to the peculiar humanitarian character which the circumstances of the country have given to the work of reform, been subordinated in the United States to brotherly kindness. Now, this right to arrange the virtues according to a scale of its own, is something which not only every age, but every nation, has claimed, and, accordingly, we find that each community, in forming its judgment of a man's character, gives a different degree of weight to different features of it. Keeping a mistress would probably, anywhere in the United States, damage a man's reputation far more seriously than fraudulent bankruptcy; while horse-stealing, which in New England would be a comparatively trifling offence, out in Montana is a far fouler thing than murder. But in the European scale, honesty still occupies the first place. Bearing this in mind, it is worth any man's while who proposes to pass judgment on the morality of any foreign country, to consider what is the impression produced on foreign opinion about American morality by the story of the Erie Railroad, by the career of Fisk, by the condition of the judicial bench in the commercial capital of the country, by the charges of corruption brought against such men as Trumbull and Fessenden at the time of the impeachment trial; by the comically prominent and beloved position which Butler has held for some years in our best moral circles, and by the condition of the civil service.

The truth is that it is almost impossible for anybody to compare one nation with another fairly, unless he possesses complete familiarity with the national life of both, and therefore can distinguish isolated facts from symptomatic facts.

The reason why some of the phenomena of American society which shock foreigners greatly, do not shock even the best Americans so much, is not that the latter have become hardened to them--though this counts for something--but that they know of various counteracting and compensating phenomena which prevent, or are sure to prevent, them in the long run from doing the mischief which they seem to threaten. In other words, they understand the checks and balances of their society as well as its tendencies. Anybody who considers these things will be careful how he denounces people whose manners differ from his own for want of spirituality or morality, and we may add that any historical student engaged in comparing the morality of the age in which he lives with that of any other age which he knows only through chronicles, will do well to exercise the same caution for the same reasons.

THE "COMIC-PAPER" QUESTION

It is recorded of a patriotic member of the Committee of Ways and Means, that after hearing from the Special Commissioner of the Revenue an elaborate and strongly fortified argument which made a deep impression on the committee in favor of a reduction of the whiskey tax, on the ground that the then rate, two dollars a gallon, could not be collected--he closed the debate, and carried the majority with him, by declaring that, for his part, he never would admit that a government which had just suppressed the greatest rebellion the world ever saw, could not collect two dollars a gallon on whiskey. A large portion of the public approaches the comic-paper problem in much the same spirit in which this gentleman approached the whiskey tax. The country has plenty of humor, and plenty of humorists. It fills whole pages of numerous magazines and whole columns of numerous newspapers with really good jokes every month. It supplies great numbers of orators and lecturers and diners-out with "little stories," which, of their kind, cannot be surpassed. There is probably no country in the world, too, in which there is so much constantly going on of the fun which does not need local knowledge or coloring to be enjoyed, but will bear exportation, and be recognized as the genuine article in any English-speaking part of the world. Moreover, there is in the real American stories an amount of suggestiveness, a power of "connotation," which cannot be affirmed of those of any other country. A very large number of them are real contributions to sociology, and of considerable value too. Besides all this, the United States possesses, what no other nation does, several professed jesters--that is, men who are not only humorous in the ordinary sense of the term, but make a business of cracking jokes, and are recognized as persons whose duty it is to take a jocose view of things. Artemus Ward, Josh Billings, and Mark Twain, and the Rev. P. V. Nasby, and one or two others of less note, are a kind of personages which no other society has produced, and could in no other society attain equal celebrity. In fact, when one examines the total annual production of jokes in the United States, one who knows nothing of the past history of the comic-paper question can hardly avoid the conclusion that such periodicals would run serious risk of being overwhelmed with "good things" and dying of plethora. Yet the melancholy fact is that several--indeed, all that have been started--have died of inanition; that is, of the absence of jokes. The last one says it offered all the great humorists in the country plenty of work, and their own terms as to pay, and failed to enlist them, and the chance jokes apparently were neither numerous enough nor good enough to keep it afloat.

Now what is the cause of this disheartening state of things? Why can the United States not have a comic paper of their own? The answers to this question vary, though of course not greatly. They are mostly given in the shape of a history, with appropriate comments, of the unsuccessful attempts made to establish comic papers; one went down because it did not sympathize with the liberal and humane movements of the day, and laughed in the pro-slavery interest; another, because it never succeeded in getting hold of a good draughtsman for its engravings; and another venture failed, among other mistakes, we are told, because it made fun of the New York *Tribune*. The explanation which finds most general favor with the public is, that while in England, France, and Germany "the great dailies" confine themselves to the serious treatment of the topics of the day, and thus leave room for the labors of *Punch*, or *Kladderadatsch*, or *Charivari*, in America all papers do their own joking; and, if it seems desirable to take a comic view of anything or anybody, take it on the spot in their own columns.

Hence any paper which starts on a comic basis alone meets with rivals in all its sober-minded contemporaries, and comes to grief. The difficulty it has to contend with is, in short, very like that which the professional laundress or baker has to contend with, owing to the fact that families are accustomed to do their own washing and bake their own bread. And, indeed, it is not unlike that with which professional writers of all kinds have to contend, owing to the readiness of clergymen, lawyers, and professors to write, while doing something else. An ordinary daily paper supplies, besides its serious disquisitions, fun enough for one average household-- sometimes in single jokes, and sometimes in the shape of "sparkle" or "spiciness" in grave articles. Often enough it is very poor stuff, but it amuses people, without turning their attention away from the sober work of life, which is the only way in which the vast body of Americans are willing to be amused. Newspaper comedians have here, what they would not have in London, a chance of letting off a joke once a day, and six or seven jokes a week is more than any comic paper is willing or able to take from any one contributor, partly owing to the need of variety in a paper given wholly to humor, and partly owing to want of space. Anybody, therefore, who has humor for sale finds a readier market among the dailies or magazines, and a far wider circle of readers, than he would in any comic paper.

The charge that our comic papers have generally opposed the friends of liberty and progress--that is the most intelligent and appreciative portion of the public--is quite true, but it does not go far to account for their failure. ***Punch*** has done this steadily ever since its establishment, without serious injury. No good cause has ever received much backing from it till it became the cause of the majority, or indeed has escaped being made the butt of its ridicule; and we confess we doubt whether "the friends of progress," using the term in what we may call its technical sense, were ever a sufficiently large body, or had ever sufficient love of fun, to make their disfavor of any great consequence. Most people in the United States who are very earnestly enlisted in the service of "a cause" look on all ridicule as "wicked," and regard with great suspicion anybody who indulges in it, whether he makes them the object of it or not. They bore with it, when turned against slavery, from one or two distinguished humorists, because its effectiveness was plain; but we doubt whether any man who had the knack of seeing the ludicrous side of things ever really won their confidence, partly owing to their own natural want of humor, and partly to their careful cultivation of a habit of solemnity of mind as the only thing that can make an "advanced" position really tenable, to say nothing of comfortable. The causes of all successes, as of all failures, in the literary world are of course various, and no doubt there is a good deal of truth in all that has been said in solution of the comic-paper problem. American humorists of the best class can find something better or more lucrative to do than writing for a comic paper; while the poor American humorists, like the poor humorists of all countries, are coarse and vulgar, even where they are not stupid.

But there is one striking difference between American society and those societies in which comic papers have succeeded which not only goes a good way to explain their failure here, but puts a better face on some of their efforts--such as their onslaughts on the friends of progress--than they seem to wear at first sight. To furnish sufficient food for fun to keep a comic paper afloat, a country must supply a good many strong social contrasts for the professional joker to play upon, and must have a large amount of reverence for social distinctions and dignities for him to shock. Two-thirds of the zest with which foreign comic papers are read is due to the fact that they caricature persons or social circles with which the mass of their readers are not thoroughly familiar, and whose habits and ways of looking at things they do not share or only partly share. A good deal of the fun in *Punch*, for instance, consists in making costermongers or cabmen quarrel with the upper classes, in ridicule of Jeames's attempts to imitate his master, of Brown's efforts to scrape acquaintance with a peer, of the absurd figure cut by the "cad" in the hunting-field, and of the folly of the city clerk in trying to dress and behave like a guardsman. In short, the point of a great number of its best jokes is made by bringing different social strata into sharp comparison. The peculiarities of Irishmen and Scotchmen also furnish rich materials to the caricaturist. He never tires of illustrating the blunders and impudence of the one and the hot patriotism and niggardliness of the other. The Irish Highlander, who denies, in a rich brogue, that any Irish are ever admitted into his regiment, and the cannie burgher from Aberdeen, who, on his return home from a visit to London, says it's an "awfu' dear place; that he hadna' been twa oors in the toon when bang went saxpence," are types which raise a laugh all over the United Kingdom, and all because, again, they furnish materials for ludicrous contrast which everybody is capable of appreciating.

Neither the Irishman, Scotchman, nor Englishman, as such, can be made to yield much fun, if sketched alone. It is when ranged alongside of each other, and measured by the English middle-class standard of propriety, that they become entertaining.

In a homogeneous society, like that of the United States, none of this material is to be found. The New Englander, to be sure, furnishes a type which differs from the Middle-States man or the Southerner or Westerner, but none of them differs enough to make him worth caricaturing. His speech, his dress, his modes of acting and thinking so nearly resemble those of his neighbors in other parts of the country that after the comic writer or draughtsman had done his best or his worst upon him, it would remain still a little doubtful where the joke came in. The Irishman, and especially the New York Irish voter, and his sister Bridget, the cook, have during the past ten years rendered more or less service as butts for caricaturists, but they are rapidly wearing out. They are not many-sided persons at best, and their characteristics have become associated in the American mind with so much that is uncomfortable and repulsive in domestic and political life, that it becomes increasingly difficult to get a native to laugh at them. It must be confessed, too, that the Irish in America have signally belied the poet's assertion, "*Coelum non animam mutant qui trans mare currunt*." There is nothing more striking in their condition than the almost complete disappearance from their character, at least in its outward manifestations, of the vivacity, politeness, kindliness, comical blundering impetuosity, and double-sightedness, out of which the Irishman of the stage and Jo Miller's Irishman who made all the bulls were manufactured in the last century. Of the other nationalities we need hardly speak, as the English-speaking public knows little of them, although the German Jew is perhaps the most durable material the comic writer has ever worked on.

The absence of class distinctions here, too, and the complete democratization of institutions during the last forty years, have destroyed the reverence and sense of mystery by shocking which the European comic paper produces some of its most tickling effects. Gladstone and Disraeli figuring as pugilists in the ring, for instance, diverts the English public, because it gives a very smart blow to the public sense of fitness, and makes a strong impression of absurdity, these two men being to the English public real dignitaries, in the strict sense of the word, and under the strongest obligations to behave properly. But a representation of Grant and Sumner as pugilists would hardly make Americans laugh, because, though absurd, it would not be nearly so absurd, or run counter to any so sharply defined standard of official demeanor. The Lord Chief-Justice playing croquet with a pretty girl owes nearly all its point, as a joke, to the popular awe of him and the mystery which surrounds his mode of life in popular eyes; a picture of Chief-Justice Chase doing the same thing would hardly excite a smile, because everybody knows him, and has known him all his life, and can have access to him at any hour of the night or day. And then it must be borne in mind that Paris and London contain all the famous men of France and England, and anybody who jokes about them is sure of having the whole public for an audience; while the best New York joke falls flat in Boston or Philadelphia, and flatter still in Cincinnati or Chicago, owing to want of acquaintance with the materials of which it is composed.

We might multiply these illustrations indefinitely, but we have probably said enough to show anyone that the field open to our comic writer is very much more restricted than that in which his European rival labors. He has, in short, to seek his jokes in character, while the European may draw largely upon manners, and it is doubtful whether character will ever supply materials for a really brilliant weekly comedian. Its points are not sufficiently salient. The American comic papers have evidently perceived the value of reverence and of violent contrast for the purposes of their profession, and this it is which leads them so constantly to select reformers and reform movements as their butts. The earnest man, intensely occupied with "a cause," comes nearer to standing in the relation to the popular mind occupied in England by the aristocrat or statesman than anybody else in America. The politician is notorious for his familiarity with all comers, and "the gentleman" has become too insignificant a person to furnish materials for a contrast; but the progressive man is sufficiently well known, and sufficiently stiff in his moral composition, to make it funny to see him in a humorous tableau.

MR. FROUDE AS A LECTURER

Mr. Froude announced that his object in coming to America was to enlighten the American public as to the true nature of Irish discontent, in such manner that American opinion, acting on Irish opinion, would reconcile the Irish to the English connection, and turn their attention to practical remedies for whatever was wrong in their condition--American opinion being now, in Irish eyes, the court of last resort in all political controversies. It is casting no reflection on the historical or literary value of his lectures to say that Mr. Froude, in proposing to himself any such undertaking, fell into error as to the kind of audience he was likely to command, and as to the nature of the impression he was likely to make. The class of persons who listen to him is one of great intelligence and respectability, but it is a class to which the Irish are not in the habit of listening, and which has already formed as unfavorable opinions about the political character of the Irish as Mr. Froude could wish. He will be surrounded during his whole tour by a public to whose utterances the Irish pay no more attention than to the preachings of Mr. Newdegate or Mr.

Whalley, and who have long ago reached, from their observation of the influence of the Irish immigration on American politics, the very conclusions for which Mr. Froude proposes to furnish historical justification. In short, he is addressing people who have either already made up their minds, or whose minds have no value for the purpose of his mission.

On the other hand, he will not reach at all the political class which panders to Irish hatred of England, and, if he does reach it, he will produce no effect on it. Not one speech the less will be uttered, or article the less written, in encourage-ment of Fenianism in consequence of anything he may say. Indeed, the idea that the Bankses will be more careful in their Congressional reports, or the Coxes or Mortons in their political harangues, either after or before election, in consequence of Mr. Froude's demonstration of the groundlessness of Fenian complaints, is one which to "the men inside politics" must be very amusing.

We think, however, we can safely go a little further than this, and say that however much light he may throw on the troubled waters of Irish history, his de-ductions will not find a ready acceptance among thinking Americans. The men who will heartily agree with him in believing that the Irish have, on the whole, only received their due, are not, as a rule, fair exponents of the national temper or of the tendencies of the national mind. Those who listened on Friday night last to his picturesque account of the Elizabethan and Cromwellian attempts to pacify Ireland, must have felt in their bones that--in spite of the cheers which greeted some of his own more eloquent and some of his bolder passages, and in particular his daunt-less way of dealing with the Drogheda Massacre--his political philosophy was not one which the average American could be got to carry home with him and ponder and embrace. Mr. Froude, it must in justice to him be said, by no means throws all the responsibility of Irish misery on Ireland. He deals out a considerable share of this responsibility to England, but then his mode of apportioning it is one which is completely opposed to most of the fundamental notions of American politics. For instance, his whole treatment of Irish history is permeated by an idea which, what-ever marks it may have left on American practice in dealing with the Indians, has no place now in American political philosophy--we mean what is called in English politics "the imperial idea"--the idea, that is, that a strong, bold, and courageous race has a sort of "natural right" to invade the territory of weak, semi-civilized, and distracted races, and undertake the task of governing them by such methods as seem best, and at such cost of life as may be necessary. This idea is a necessary product of English history; it is not likely to disappear in England as long as she possesses such a school for soldiers and statesmen as is furnished by India. Indeed, she could not stay in India without some such theory to support her troops, but it is not one which will find a ready acceptance here. American opinion has, within the last twenty years, run into the very opposite extreme, and now maintains with some tenacity the right even of barbarous communities to be let alone and allowed to work out their own salvation or damnation in their own way. There is little or no faith left in this country in the value of superimposed civilization, or of "superior minds," or of higher organization, while there is a deep suspicion of, or we might say there is deep hostility toward, all claims to rule based on alleged superiority of race or creed or class. We doubt if Mr. Froude could have hit on a more unpalatable mode, or a mode more likely to clash with the prevailing tendencies of American opinion, of defending English rule in Ireland than the argument that, Englishmen being stronger and wiser than Irishmen, Irishmen ought to submit to have themselves governed on English ideas whether they like it or not. He has produced this argument already in England, and it has elicited there a considerable amount of indignant protest. We are forced to say of it here that it is likely to do great mischief, over and above the total defeat of Mr. Froude's object in coming to this country. The Irish in America are more likely to be exasperated by it than the Irish at home, and we feel sure that no native American will ever venture to use it to an Irish audience.

There is one other point to which Mr. Froude's attention ought to be called, as likely seriously to diminish the political weight of his exposition of the causes of Irish discontent. The sole justification of a conquest, even of a conquest achieved over barbarians by a civilized people, is that it supplies good government--that is, protection for life and property. Unless it does this, no picture, however dark, of the discords and disorder and savagery of the conquered can set the conqueror right at the bar of civilized opinion. Therefore, the shocking and carefully darkened pictures of the social and political degradation of the native Irish in the fifteenth, sixteenth, and seventeenth centuries with which Mr. Froude is furnishing us, are available for English vindication only on the supposition that the invasion, even if it destroyed liberty, brought with it law and order. But according to Mr. Froude's eloquent confession, it brought nothing of the kind.

Queen Elizabeth made the first serious attempt to subjugate Ireland, but she did it, Mr. Froude tells us, with only a handful of English soldiers--who acted as auxiliaries to Irish clans engaged on the queen's instigation in mutual massacre. After three years of this sort of thing, the whole southern portion of the island was reduced, to use Mr. Froude's words, "to a smoking wilderness," men, women, and children having been remorselessly slaughtered; but no attempt whatever was then made to establish either courts or police, or any civil rule of any kind. Society was left in a worse condition than before. Why was this? Because, says Mr. Froude, the English Constitution made no provision for the maintenance of a standing army for any such purpose.

The second attempt was made by Cromwell. He slaughtered the garrisons of Drogheda and Wexford, and scattered the armies of the various Irish factions, but he made no more attempt to police the island than Elizabeth. The only mode of establishing order resorted to by the Commonwealth was the wholesale confiscation of the land, and its distribution among the officers and soldiers of the army, the natives of all ages and sexes being driven into Connaught. The "policing" was then left to be done by the new settlers, each man with the strong hand, on his own account. The third attempt was made by William III., who also followed the Cromwellian plan, and left the island to be governed during the following century by the military adventurers who had entered into possession of the soil.

The excuse for not endeavoring to set up an honest and efficient government remained the same in all three cases; the absence of an army, or occupation elsewhere. In other words, the conquest from first to last wanted the only justification which any conquest can have. England found the Irish much in the same stage of social and political progress in which Caesar found the Gauls, destitute of nearly all the elements of political organization; but instead of founding a political system, and maintaining it, she interfered for century after century only to subjugate and lay waste, and set the natives by the ears. Mr. Froude's answer to this is, that if the Irish had been better men they could easily have driven the English out, which is perhaps a good reason for not bestowing much pity on the Irish, but it is not a good reason for telling the Irish they ought not to hate England. No pity can be made welcome which is ostentatiously mingled with contempt. It is quite true, to our minds, that during the last fifty years England has supplied the Irish with a better government than the Irish could provide for themselves within the next century at least.

There is no doubt of the substantial value of the English connection to Ireland **now**; but there is just as little that in the past history of this connection there is reason enough for Irish suspicion and dislike. The tenacity of the Irish memory, too, is one of the great political defects and misfortunes of the race. Inability to forget past "wrongs" in the light of present prosperity, is a sure sign of the absence of the political sense; and that the Irish are wanting in the political sense no candid man can deny. That they are really still, to a considerable extent, in the tribal stage of progress, there is little doubt. But they are surrounded by ideas, and institutions, and influences which make it useless to try to raise them out of that stage by the "imperial" method of government, or, in other words, by trying to persuade them that they have richly deserved all their misfortunes, and that the best thing they can do is to let a superior race mould their destinies. If it were possible for Englishmen to be a little more patient with their weaknesses, to yield a little more to the childish vanities and aspirations which form the nearest approach they have yet made to a feeling of nationality, and take upon themselves in word as well as in deed their share of the horrible burdens of Irish history, it would do more toward winning them Irish confidence than anything Americans are ever likely to say.

MR. HORACE GREELEY

There has been something almost tragic about the close of Mr. Greeley's career. After a life of, on the whole, remarkable success and prosperity, he fell finally under the weight of accumulated misfortunes. Nobody who heard him declare that "he accepted the Cincinnati Convention and its consequences," but must be struck by the illustration of what is called "the irony of fate," which nearly everything that occurred afterwards affords. His nomination, from whatever point of view we look at it, was undoubtedly a high honor. The manner in which it was received down to the Baltimore Convention was very flattering. Whether it was a proper thing to "beat Grant" or not, that so large and so shrewd a body of his countrymen should have thought Mr. Greeley the man to do it was a great compliment. It found him, too, in possession of all the influence which the successful pursuit of his own calling could give a man--the most powerful editor in the Union, surrounded by friends and admirers, feared or courted by nearly everybody in public life, and in the full enjoyment of widespread popular confidence in his integrity. In six short months he was well-nigh undone. He had endured a humiliating defeat, which seemed to him to indicate the loss of what was his dearest possession, the affection of the American people; he had lost the weight in public affairs which he had built up by thirty years of labor; he saw his property and, as he thought, that of his friends diminished by the attempt to give him a prize which he had in his own estimation fairly earned, and, though last not least, he found his home invaded by death, and one of the strongest of the ties which bind a man to this earth broken. It would not be wonderful if, under these circumstances, the coldest and toughest of men should lie down and die. But Mr. Greeley was neither cold nor tough. He was keenly sensitive both to praise and blame. The applause of even paltry men gladdened him, and their censure stung him. Moreover, he had that intense longing for reputation as a man of action by which men of the closet are so often torn. In spite of all that his writing brought him in reputation, he writhed under the popular belief that he could do nothing but write, and he spent the flower of his years trying to convince the public that it was mistaken about him. It was to this we owed whatever was ostentatious in his devotion to farming, and in his interest in the manufacturing industry of the country. It was to this, too, that he owed his keen and lifelong desire for office, and, in part at least, his activity in getting offices for other people.

Office-seekers have become in the United States so ridiculous and so contemptible a class, that a man can hardly seek a place in the public service without incurring a certain amount of odium; and perhaps nothing did more damage to Mr. Greeley's reputation than his anxiety to be put in places of trust or dignity. And yet it is doubtful if many men seek office with more respectable motives than his. For pecuniary emolument he cared nothing; but he did pine all his life long for some conspicuous recognition of his capacity for the conduct of affairs, and he never got it. The men who have nominations to bestow either never had confidence enough in his judgment or ability to offer him anything which he would have thought worthy of his expectations when there was the least chance of their choice receiving a popular ratification. They disliked him, as politicians are apt to dislike an editor in the political arena, as a man who, in having a newspaper at his back, is sure not to play their game fairly. The consequence was that he was constantly irritated by finding how purely professional his influence was, or, in other words, what a mortifying disproportion existed between his editorial and his personal power. The first revelation the public had of the bitterness of his disappointment on this score was caused by the publication of the famous Seward letter, and the surprise it caused was perhaps the highest compliment Mr. Greeley ever received. It showed with what success he had prevented his private griefs from affecting his public action, and people are always ready to forgive ambition as an "infirmity of noble minds," even when they do not feel disposed to reward it.

Unfortunately for Mr. Greeley, however, he never could persuade himself that the public was of the same mind as the politicians regarding his personal capacity. He persisted to the last in believing himself the victim of their envy, hatred, and malice, and looking with unabated hope to some opportunity of obtaining a verdict on his merits as a man of action, in which his widespread popularity and his long and laborious teachings would fairly tell. The result of the Cincinnati Convention, which his friends and emissaries from this city went out to prepare, but which perhaps neither he nor they in the beginning ventured to hope for, seemed to promise him at last the crown and consummation of a life's longings, and he received it with almost childlike joy. The election was, therefore, a crushing blow. It was not, perhaps, the failure to get the presidency that was hardest to bear--for this might have been accompanied by such a declaration of his fitness for the presidency as would have sweetened the remainder of his years--it was the contemptuous greatness of his opponent's majority which was killing. It dissipated the illusion of half a lifetime on the one point on which illusions are dearest--a man's exact place in the estimation of his countrymen. Very few--even of those whose fame rests on the most solid foundation of achievement--ever ask to have this ascertained by a positive test without dread or misgiving, or face the test without a strain, which the nerves of old men are often ill fitted to bear. That Mr. Greeley's nerves were unequal to the shock of failure we now know. But it needed no intimate acquaintance with him to see that the card in which he announced, two days after the election, that he would thereafter be a simple editor, would seek office no more, and would confine himself to the production of a candid and judicial-minded paper, must have been written in bitterness of spirit for which this world had no balm.

In addition to the deceptions caused by his editorial influence, Mr. Greeley had others to contend with, more subtle, but not less potent. The position of the editor of a leading daily paper is one which, in our time, is hardly possible for the calmest and most candid man to fill without having his judgment of himself perverted by flattery. Our age is intensely commercial; it is not the dry-goods man or the grain merchant only who has goods for sale, but the poet, the orator, the scholar, the philosopher, and the politician. We are all, in a measure, seeking a market for our wares. What we desire, therefore, above all things, is a good advertising medium, or, in other words, a good means of making known to all the world where our store is and what we have to sell. This means the editor of a daily paper can furnish to anybody he pleases. He is consequently the object of unceasing adulation from a crowd of those who shrink from fighting the slow and doubtful battle of life in the open field, and crave the kindly shelter of editorial plaudits, "puffs," and "mentions." He finds this adulation offered freely, and by all classes and conditions, without the least reference to his character or talents or antecedents. What wonder if it turns the heads of unworthy men, and begets in them some of the vices of despots--their unscrupulousness, their cruelty, and their impudence. What wonder, too, if it should have thrown off his balance a man like Mr. Greeley, whose head was not strong, whose education was imperfect, and whose self-confidence had been fortified by a brave and successful struggle with adversity.

Of his many private virtues, of his kind-heartedness, his generosity, his sympathy with all forms of suffering and anxiety, we do not need to speak. His career, too, has little in it to point any moral that is not already trite and familiar. The only lesson we can gather from it with any clearness is the uncertainty of this world, and all that it contains, and the folly of seeking the presidency. Nobody can hope to follow in his footsteps. He began life as a kind of editor of which he was one of the last specimens, and which will shortly be totally extinct--the editor who fought as the man-at-arms of the party. This kind of work Mr. Greeley did with extraordinary earnestness and vehemence and success--so much success that a modern newspaper finally grew up around him, in spite of him, almost to his surprise, and often to his embarrassment. The changed condition of journalism, the substitution of the critical for the party views of things, he never wholly accepted, and his frequent personal appearance in his columns, under the signature of "H. G." hurling defiance at his enemies or exposing their baseness, showed how stifling he found the changed atmosphere. He was fast falling behind his age when he died. New men, and new issues, and new processes, which he either did not understand at all or only understood imperfectly, crowded upon him. If the dazzling prize of the presidency had not been held before his eyes, we should probably have witnessed his gradual but certain retirement into well-won repose. Those who opposed him most earnestly must now regret sincerely that in his last hours he should have known the bitterness of believing, what was really not true, that the labors of his life, which were largely devoted to good causes, had not met the appreciation they merited at the hands of his countrymen. It is for his own sake, as well as that of the public, greatly to be regretted that he should not have lived until the smoke of the late conflict had cleared away.

THE MORALS AND MANNERS OF THE KITCHEN

Mr. Froude's attempt to secure from the American public a favorable judgment on the dealings of England with Ireland has had one good result--though we fear only one--in leading to a little closer examination of the real state of American opinion about Irish grievances than it has yet received. He will go back to England with the knowledge--which he evidently did not possess when he came here--that the great body of intelligent Americans care very little about the history of "the six hundred years of wrong," and know even less than they care, and could not be induced, except by a land-grant, or a bounty, or a drawback, to acquaint themselves with it; that those of them who have ever tried to form an opinion on the Anglo-Irish controversy have hardly ever got farther than a loose notion that England had most likely behaved like a bully all through, but that her victim was beyond all question an obstreperous and irreclaimable ruffian, whose ill-treatment must be severely condemned by the moralist, but over whom no sensible man can be expected to weep or sympathize.

The agencies which have helped to form the popular idea of the English political character are well known; those which have helped to deprive the Irish of American sympathy--and which, if Mr. Froude had judiciously confined himself to describing the efforts made by England to promote Irish well-being *now*, would probably have made his lectures very successful--are more obscure. We ourselves pointed out one of the most prominent, and probably most powerful--the conduct of the Irish servant-girl in the American kitchen. To this must of course be added the specimen of "home rule" to which the country has been treated in this city; but we doubt if this latter has really exercised as much influence on American opinion as some writers try to make out. A community which has produced Butler, Banks, Parker, Bullock, Tweed, Tom Fields, Oakey Hall, Fernando Wood, Barnard, and scores of others whom we might name, as the results of good Protestant and Anglo-Saxon breeding, cannot really be greatly shocked by the bad workings of Celtic blood and Catholic theology in the persons of Peter B. Sweeny, Billy McMullen, Jimmy O'Brien, Reddy the Blacksmith, or Judge McCunn. It is in the kitchen that the Irish iron has entered into the American soul; and it is in the kitchen that a great triumph was prepared for Mr. Froude, had he been a judicious man. The memory of burned steaks, of hard-boiled potatoes, of smoked milk, would have done for him what no state papers, or records, or correspondence of the illustrious dead can ever do; it had prepared the American mind to believe the very worst he could say of Irish turbulence and disorder. Not one of his auditors but could find in his own experience of Irish cooking circumstances which would probably have led him to accept without question the execution of Silken Thomas, the massacre of Drogheda, or even the Penal Laws, as perfectly justifiable exercises of authority, and would certainly have made it easy for him to believe that English rule in Ireland at the present day is beneficent beyond example.

Nevertheless, we are constrained to say that in our opinion a great deal of the odium which surrounds Bridget, and which has excited so much prejudice, not only against her countrymen, but against her ancestors, in American eyes, has a very insufficient foundation in reason. There are three characters in which she is the object of public suspicion and dislike--(1) as a cook; (2) as a party to a contract; (3) as a member of a household. The charges made against her in all of these have been summed up in a recent attack on her in the ***Atlantic Monthly***, as "a lack of every quality which makes service endurable to the employer, or a wholesome life for the servant."

And the same article charges her with "proving herself, in obedience, fidelity, care, and accuracy, the inferior of every kind of servant known to modern society." Of course, there is hardly a family in the country which has not had, in its own experience, illustrations of the extravagance of these charges. There is probably nobody who has long kept servants, who has not had Irish servants who were obedient, faithful, careful, and even accurate in a remarkable degree. But then it must be admitted that this indictment is a tolerably fair rendering, if not of the actual facts of the case, at least of the impression the facts have left on the mind of the average employer. This impression, however, needs correction, as a few not very recondite considerations will show.

As a cook, Bridget is an admitted failure. But cooking is, it is now generally acknowledged, very much an affair of instinct, and this instinct seems to be very strong in some races and very weak in others, though why the French should have it highly developed, and the Irish be almost altogether deprived of it, is a question which would require an essay to itself. No amount of teaching will make a person a good cook who is not himself fond of good food and has not a delicate palate, for it is the palate which must test the value of rules. We may deduce from this the conclusion, which experience justifies, that women are not naturally good cooks. They have had the cookery of the world in their hands for several thousand years, but all the marked advances in the art, and indeed all that can be called the cultivation of it, have been the work of men. Whatever zeal women have displayed in it, and whatever excellence they have achieved in it, have been the result of influences in no way gastronomic, and which we might perhaps call emotional, such as devotion to male relatives, or a desire to minister to the pleasure of men in general. Few or no women cook a dinner in an artistic spirit, and their success in doing it is nearly always the result of affection or loyalty--which is of course tantamount to saying that female cookery as a whole is, and always has been, comparatively poor.

As a proof of this, we may mention the fact--for fact we think it is--that the art of cooking among women has declined at any given time or place--in the Northern States of the Union, for instance--*pari passu*, with the growth of female independence. That is, as the habit or love of ministering to men's tastes has become weaker, the interest in cookery has fallen off. There are no such cooks among native American women now as there were fifty years ago; and passages in foreign cookery books which assume the existence among women of strong interest in their husbands' and brothers' likings, and strong desire to gratify them, furnish food for merriment in American households. Bridget, therefore, can plead, first of all, the general incapacity of women as cooks; and, secondly, the general falling off in the art under the influence of the new ideas. It may be that she *ought* to cultivate assiduously or with enthusiasm a calling which all the other women of the country ostentatiously despise, but she would be more than human if she did so. She imitates American women as closely as she can, and cannot live on the same soil without imbibing their ideas; and unhappily, as in all cases of imitation, vices are more easily and earlier caught than virtues.

She can make, too, an economical defence of the most powerful kind, to the attacks on her in this line, and it is this: that whether her cooking be bad or good, she offers it without deception or subterfuge, at a fair rate, and without compulsion; that nobody who does not like her dishes need eat them; and that her defects of taste or training can only be fairly made a cause of hatred and abuse when she does work badly, which somebody else is waiting to do better, if she would get out of the way. She has undertaken the task of cooking for the American nation, not of her own motion, but simply and solely because the American nation could find nobody else to do it. She does not, therefore, occupy the position of a broken-down or incompetent artist, but of a volunteer at a fire, or a passer-by when you are lying in the ditch with your leg broken.

The plain truth of the matter is, that the whole native population of the United States has almost suddenly, and with one accord, refused to perform for hire any of the services usually called "menial" or indoor. The men have found other more productive fields of industry, and the women, under the influence of the prevailing theory of life, have resolved to accept any employment at any wages sooner than do other people's housework. The result has been a demand for trained servants which the whole European continent could not supply if it would, and which has proved so intense that it has drawn the peasantry out of the fields *en masse* from the one European country in which the peasantry was sufficiently poor to be tempted, and spoke or understood the American language. No such phenomenon has ever been witnessed before. No country before has ever refused to do its own "chores," and called in an army of foreigners for the purpose. To complain bitterly of their want of skill is therefore, under the circumstances, almost puerile, from an economical point of view; while, to anyone who looks at the matter as a moralist, it is hard to see why Bridget, doing the work badly in the kitchen, is any more a contemptible object than the American sewing-girl killing herself in a garret at three dollars a week, out of devotion to "the principle of equality."

As a party to a contract, Bridget's defects are very strongly marked. Her sense of the obligation of contracts is feeble. The reason why this particular vice excites so much odium in her case is, that the inconveniences of her breaches of contract are greater than those of almost any other member of the community. They touch us in our most intimate social relations, and cause us an amount of mental anguish out of all proportion to their real importance. But her spirit about contracts is really that of the entire community in which she lives. Her way of looking at her employer is, we sincerely believe, about the way of looking at him common among all employees. The only real restraint on laborers of any class among us nowadays is the difficulty of finding another place. Whenever it becomes as easy for clerks, draughtsmen, mechanics, and the like to "suit themselves" as it is for cooks or housemaids, we find them as faithless. Native mechanics and seamstresses are just as perfidious as Bridget, but incur less obloquy, because their faithlessness causes less annoyance; but they have no more regard in making their plans for the interest or wishes of their employer than she has, and they all take the "modern view" of the matter. What makes her so fond of change is that she lives in a singularly restless society, in which everybody is engaged in a continual struggle to "better himself"--her master, in nine cases out of ten, setting her an example of dislike to steady industry and slow gains. Moreover, domestic service is a kind of employment which, if not sweetened by personal affection, is extraordinarily full of wear and tear. In it there is no real end to the day, and in small households, the pursuit and oversight, and often the "nagging," of the employer, or, in other words, the presence of an exacting, semi-hostile, and slightly contemptuous person is constant. This and confinement in a half-dark kitchen produce that nervous crisis which sends male mechanics and other male laborers, engaged in monotonous callings, off "on a spree." In Bridget's case it works itself off by a change of place, with a few days of squalid repose among "her own people" in a tenement-house.

As regards her general bearing as a member of a household, she has to contend with three great difficulties--ignorance of civilized domestic life, for which she is no more to blame than Russian moujiks; difference of race and creed on the part of her employer (and this is one which the servants of no other country have to contend with); and lastly, the strong contempt for domestic service felt and manifested by all that portion of the American population with which she comes in contact, and to which it is her great ambition to assimilate herself. Those who have ever tried the experiment of late years of employing a native American as a servant, have, we believe, before it was over, generally come to look on Bridget as the personification of repose, if not of comfort; and those who have to call on native Americans, even occasionally, for services of a quasi-personal character, such as those of express-men, hotel clerks, plumbers, we believe are anxious to make their intercourse with these gentlemen as brief as possible. Most expressmen are natives, and are freemen of intelligence and capacity, but they carry your trunk into your hall with the air of convicts doing forced labor for a tyrannical jailer. If the spirit in which they discharge their duties--and they are specimens of a large class--were to make its way into our kitchens, society would go to pieces.

In short, Bridget is the legitimate product of our economical, political, and moral condition. We have called her, in our extremity, to do duties for which she is not trained, and having got her here have surrounded her with influences and ideas which American society has busied itself for fifty years in fostering and spreading, and which, taking hold of persons in her stage of development, work mental and moral ruin. The things which American life and manners preach to her are not patience, sober-mindedness, faithfulness, diligence, and honesty, and eagerness for physical enjoyment. Whenever the sound of the new gospel which is to win the natives back to the ancient and noble ways is heard in the land, it is fair to expect that it will not find her ears wholly closed, and that when the altar of duty is again set up by her employers, she will lay on it attractive beefsteaks, potatoes done to a turn, make libations of delicious soup, and will display remarkable fertility in "sweets," and an extreme fondness for washing, and learn to grow old in one family.

JOHN STUART MILL

Mr. Mill was, in many respects, one of the most singular men ever produced by English society. His father was a prominent member of the small sect or coterie of Benthamites, whose attempts to reform the world, during the whole of the earlier part of the present century, furnished abundant matter for ridicule to the common run of politicians and social philosophers; and this ridicule was heightened, as the years rolled on, by the extraordinary jargon which their master adopted for the communication of his discoveries to the world. The author of the "Defence of Usury," of the "Fragment on Government," and of the "Book of Fallacies," had, however, secured a reputation very early in his career which his subsequent eccentricities could not shake, but the first attempts of his disciples to catch the public ear were not fortunate. Macaulay's smart review of James Mill's book on "Government" gives a very fair expression to the common feeling about them in English literary and political circles during John Stuart's boyhood. About the value of the father's labors as a mental philosopher there are of course a variety of opinions, but he gave two proofs of capacity for the practical work of life which there was no gainsaying. He came to London an obscure man of humble origin, but managed, without ever having been in India, and at a period when authors were held in much less esteem by politicians than they were at a later period, to produce such an impression of his knowledge of Indian affairs, by his elaborate history of that country, on the minds of the Directors of the Company, that they gave him an important office in the India House, and this, too, in spite of the fact that he lived in a circle generally considered visionary--answering, in fact, in some degree to what we call the "long-haired people." Besides this, he himself personally gave his son an education which made him, perhaps, all things considered, the most accomplished man of his age, and without help from the universities or any other institution of learning. The son grew up with a profound reverence for his father as a scholar and thinker, and rarely lost an opportunity of expressing it, though, curiously enough, he began very early to look on Bentham, the head of the school, with a critical eye. The young man's course was, however, still more remarkable than the father's.

Although brought up in a narrow coterie holding peculiar and somewhat unpopular opinions, and displaying, from his first entrance in life, as intense hostility as it was in his nature to feel against anything, against the English universities as then organized and conducted, though they were the centre of English culture and indeed one might say of intellectual activity, he saw himself, before he reached middle life, the most potent influence known to educated Englishmen, and perhaps that which has most contributed to the late grave changes in English public opinion on several of the leading social and political problems. Indeed, it is not too much to say that his writings produced a veritable ***debacle*** in the English mind. The younger generation were a good deal stirred by Carlyle; but Carlyle, after all, only woke people up, and made them look out of the window to see what was the matter, after which most of them went to bed again and slept comfortably. His cries were rather too inarticulate to furnish anything like a new gospel, and he never took hold of the intellectual class. But Mill did. The "Logic" and "Political Economy," as reinforced and expounded by his earlier essays, were generally accepted by the younger men as the teachings of a real master, and even those who fully accepted neither his mental philosophy nor his social economy, acknowledged that the day of old things was passing away under his preaching. His method, however, as applied to politics, was not original--in fact, it was Bentham's.

Bentham, who was perhaps, in the field of jurisprudence, the most destructive critic that ever appeared, had the merit which in his day was somewhat novel among reformers, and marked him out as something very different from Continental radicals--of being also highly constructive. Indeed, his labors in providing substitutes for what he sought to overthrow are among the most curious, and, we might add, valuable monuments of human industry and ingenuity. His proposed reforms were based, too, on a theory of human nature which differed from that in use among a large number of radicals in our day in being perfectly sound, that is, in perfect accordance with observed facts, as far as it went. But it did not go nearly far enough. It did not embrace the whole of human nature, or even the greater part of it, and for the simple reason, which Mr. Mill himself has pointed out in his analysis of Bentham's character, that its author was almost entirely wanting in sympathy and imagination. A very large proportion of the springs of human action were unknown or incomprehensible to him.

The result was that, although he exerted a powerful influence on English law reform by his exposure of specific abuses, he made little impression on English sociology, properly so called. This was in part due to his narrowness of view, and in part to the absence of an interpreter, none of his followers having attempted to put his wisdom into readable shape, except Dumont, and he only partially and in French. The application of his method to the work of general reform was indeed left to Mr. Mill, who brought to the task an amount of culture to which Bentham could make no claim, and a large share of the sympathy of which there was also so little in Bentham's composition, and a style which, for expository and didactic purposes, has perhaps never been surpassed. Moreover, Mr. Mill lost no time, as most men do, in maturing. He was a full-blown philosopher at twenty-five, and discourses in his earliest essays with almost the same measure, circumspection, and gravity exhibited in the latest of his works, and with all the Benthamite precision and attention to limitations.

He was, however, wanting, as his master was, in imagination, and wanting, too, in what we may call, though not in any bad sense, the animal side of man's nature. He suffered in his treatment of all the questions of the day from excess of culture and deficiency of blood. He understood and allowed for men's errors of judgment and for their ignorance, and for their sloth and indifference; but of appreciation of the force of their passions his speculations contain little sign. For instance, he was the first to point out the fact that the principle of competition, the eager desire to sell, which furnishes the motive power of the English and American social organization, is almost unknown and unfelt among the greater part of mankind, but his remedy for redundancy of population, and his lamentations over "the subjection of women," are those of a recluse or a valetudinarian.

His influence as a political philosopher may be said to have stood highest after the appearance of the "Political Economy." He had, then, perhaps the most remarkable following of hard-headed men which any English philosopher was ever able to show. But the reverence of his disciples waned somewhat rapidly after he began to take a more active part in the treatment of the questions of the day. His "representative government," valuable as it was as a philosophical discussion, offered no solution of the problem then pressing on the public minds in England, which bitter Radicals or Conservatives could consider comforting. The plan of having the number of a man's votes regulated by his calling and intelligence was thoroughly Benthamite. It was as complete and logical as a proposition in Euclid, and in 1825 would have looked attractive; but in 1855 the power of doing this nice work had completely passed out of everybody's hands--indeed, the desire of political perfection had greatly abated. His lofty and eloquent plaints on the decline of social freedom helped to strengthen the charge of want of practicalness, which in our day is so injurious to a man's political influence, and when he entered Parliament, although he disappointed none of those who best understood him, the outside multitude, who had begun to look on him as a prophet, were somewhat chagrined that he was not readier in parrying the thrusts of the trained gladiators of the House of Commons. It was the book on the "Subjection of Women," however, which most shook the allegiance of his more educated followers, because it was marked by the widest departures from his own rules of thinking. It would be impossible to find any justification in his other works for the doctrine that women are inferior to men for the same reason that male serfs are inferior to their masters. His refusal to consider difference of sex as even one probable cause of women's inferiority to men in mental and moral characteristics, was something for which few of his disciples were prepared, or which they ever got over; and indeed his whole treatment of the question of sex showed, in the opinion of many, a constitutional incapacity to deal with the gravest problems of social economy.

The standing of Mr. Mill as a mental philosopher appears to be very differently estimated by late critics and opponents and by himself, whether we consider the extent of his influence, or the relations of his doctrines to his nation and time; and there is a most singular inversion in these estimates of what we should naturally expect from friend and foe--an estimate of Mill's position and influence by his opponents, which, compared to his own, seems greatly exaggerated. For example, Dr. McCosh, a thorough-going opponent, regards Mill's influence as the most active and effective philosophical force now alive in Great Britain, the strongest current of philosophic thought even at Oxford; and M. Taine, who some years ago discovered at Oxford that the British nation was not wanting in "general ideas" or principles in its modes of thought above the requirements of the accountant and assayer, found these principles in a really living English philosophy, which has brought forth one of M. Taine's most elaborate critical studies in his work on "Intelligence." In contrast with these estimates, we have from Mr. Mill himself the opinion, in a letter to M. Taine, that his views are not especially English, and that they have not been so since the philosophical reaction in Scotland, Germany, and later in England, against Hume; that when his "System of Logic" was written he "stood almost alone in his opinions; and though they have met with a degree of sympathy which he by no means expected, we may still count in England twenty *a priori* and spiritualist philosophers for every partisan of the doctrine of Experience."

This estimate of his own influence and of the importance to metaphysical discussion at the present time of the philosophy he "adopted" is entitled to much more consideration than ought in general to be allowed for an opinion inspired by the ambition, the enthusiasm, the disappointments, or even the modesty of a philosophical thinker. Nevertheless, the far different opinion of his standing as a metaphysician which his critics entertain is undoubtedly more correct, though in a sense which was not so clearly apparent to him. They see clearly that a philosophy of which he was not the founder, and never pretended to be, has gained through his writings a hold, not only on English speculation, but on that of the civilized world, which it did not acquire even in England when it was an especially English philosophy, as it was "in the first half of the eighteenth century, from the time of Locke to that of the reaction against Hume."

What, then, is it in Mill's philosophical writings that has given him this eminence as a thinker? Two qualities, we think, very rarely combined: a philosophical style which for clearness and cogency has, perhaps, never been surpassed, and a conscientious painstaking, with a seriousness of conviction, and an earnestness of purpose which did not in general characterize the thinkers whose views he adopted. It was by bringing to the support of doctrines previously regarded as irreligious a truly religious spirit that Mill acquired in part the influence and respect which have given him his eminence as a thinker. He thus redeemed the word "utility" and the utilitarian doctrine of morals from the ill repute they had, for "the greatest happiness principle" was with him a religious principle. An equally important part of his influence is doubtless due to the thoroughness of his early training--the education received from his father's instruction--which, as we have said, has made him truly regarded as the most accomplished of modern dialecticians.

To these grounds of influence may be added, so far as his influence on English thought is concerned, the fact that he was not a metaphysician in a positive fashion, though he dealt largely with metaphysical topics. He represented the almost instinctive aversion to metaphysics, as such, which has characterized the English since the time of Newton and Locke, we might also say since the time of Bacon. Metaphysics, to pass current in England, has now to be baptized and become part of the authoritative religious instruction, else it is foreign and barbarous to the English matter-of-fact ways of thinking. Mill's "System of Logic" was not intended as a system of *philosophy* in the German, French, or even Scotch sense of the term. It is not through the *a priori* establishment or refutation of highest principles that experiential, inductive, fact-proven principles of science are regarded or tested by the unmetaphysical English mind. Metaphysical doctrines prevail, it is true, in England, to the extent, probably, that Mr. Mill estimates--twenty to one of its thinkers holding to some such views. Yet it would be a misconception to suppose these to be products of modern English *thought*. They are rather preserves, tabooed, interdicted to discussion, not the representatives of its living thought.

Mr. Mill estimated the worth of contemporary thinkers in accordance with this almost instinctive distrust of rational "illumination;" setting Archbishop Whately, for example, as a thinker, above Sir W. Hamilton, for his services to philosophy, on account of "the number of true and valuable thoughts" which he originated and put into circulation, not as parts of a system, but as independent truths of sagacious or painstaking observation and reflection. It is by such a standard that Mr. Mill would doubtless wish to be judged, and by it he would be justly placed above all, or nearly all, of his contemporaries. Nevertheless, as a conscientious student of metaphysics he held in far higher esteem than is shown in general by English thinkers the powers peculiar to the metaphysician--the ability and disposition to follow out into their consequences, and to concatenate in a system the assumption of *a priori* principles. Descartes, Leibnitz, Comte, and, as an exceptional English thinker, even Mr. Spencer, receive commendation from him on this account. It is clear, however, that his respect for this talent was of the sort which does not aspire to imitate what is admired.

PANICS

It is impossible to see, much less experience, a financial panic without an almost appalling consciousness that a new and terrible form of danger and distress has been added in comparatively recent times to the list of those by which human life is menaced or perplexed. Any one who stood on Wall Street, or in the gallery of the Stock Exchange last Thursday and Friday and Saturday (1873), and saw the mad terror, we might almost say the brute terror like that by which a horse is devoured who has a pair of broken shafts hanging to his heels, or a dog flying from a tin saucepan attached to his tail, with which great crowds of men rushed to and fro, trying to get rid of their property, almost begging people to take it from them at any price, could hardly avoid feeling that a new plague had been sent among men; that there was an impalpable, invisible force in the air, robbing them of their wits, of which philosophy had not as yet dreamt. No dog was ever so much alarmed by the clatter of the saucepan as hundreds seemed to be by the possession of really valuable and dividend-paying securities; and no horse was ever more reckless in extricating himself from the *debris* of a broken carriage than these swarms of acute and shrewd traders in divesting themselves of their possessions. Hundreds must really, to judge by their conduct, have been so confused by terror and anxiety as to be unable to decide whether they desired to have or not to have, to be poor or rich. If a Roman or a man of the Middle Ages had been suddenly brought into view of the scene, he would have concluded without hesitation that a ruthless invader was coming down the island; that his advanced guard was momentarily expected; and that anybody found by his forces in possession of Western Union, or Harlem, or Lake Shore, or any other paying stock or bond, would be subjected to cruel tortures, if not put to death. For neither the Roman nor the Mediaeval could understand a rich man's being terrified by anything but armed violence. Seneca enumerates as the three great sources of anxiety in life the fear of want, of disease, and of oppression by the powerful, and he pronounces the last the greatest. If he had seen Wall-Street brokers and bankers last week trying to get rid of stocks and bonds, he could not of course have supposed that they were poor or feared poverty; he would have judged from their physical activity that they were in perfect health, so that he would have been driven to the conclusion that some barbarian host, commanded by Sitting Bull or Red Cloud, was entering the city, and was breathing out threatenings and slaughter against the owners of personal property. If you had tried to explain to him that there was no conqueror at the gates, that the fear of violence was almost unknown in our lives, that each man in that struggling crowd enjoyed an amount of security against force in all its forms which no Roman Senator could ever count upon, and that the terror he witnessed was caused by precisely the same agency as the flight of an army before it has been beaten, or, in other words, by "panic," he would have gazed at you in incredulous amazement. He would have said that panic in an army was caused by the sudden dissolution of the bonds of discipline, by each soldier's losing his confidence that his comrades and his officers would stand their ground; but these traders, he would have added, are not subject to discipline; they do not belong to an organization of any kind; each buys and sells for himself; he has his property there in that tin box, and if nobody is going to rob him what is frightening him? Why is he pale and trembling? Why does he run and shout and weep, and ask people to give him a trifle, only a trifle, for all he possesses and let him go?

If you were then to set about explaining to Seneca that the way the god Pan worked confusion in our day in the commercial world was by destroying "credit," you would find yourself brought suddenly face to face with one of the most striking differences between ancient and modern, or, even as we have said, mediaeval society. The most prominent and necessary accompaniment or incident of property in the ancient world was possession. What a man owned he held. His wealth was in his farm, or his house, or his granary, or his ships. He could hardly separate the idea of property from that of possession, and the state of society strengthened the association. The frugal man hoarded, and when he was terrified he buried his money, a practice to which we owe the preservation of the greater portion of the old coins now in our collections. The influence of this sense of insecurity, of the constant fear of invasion or violence, lasted long enough in all Continental countries, as Mr. Bagehot has recently pointed out, to prevent the establishment of banks of issue until very lately. The prospect of war was so constantly in men's minds that no bank could make arrangements for the run which would surely follow the outbreak of hostilities, and, in view of this contingency, nobody would be willing to hold paper promises to pay in lieu of gold and silver.

It is therefore in England and America, the two countries possessing not only most commercial enterprise, but most security against invasion, that the paper money has come into earliest and widest use. To the paper of the banks have been added the checks and bills of exchange of private individuals, until money proper plays a greatly diminishing part in the operations of commerce. Goods are exchanged and debts paid by a system of balancing claims against claims, which really has almost ceased to rest on money at all. So that a man may be a very rich man in our day, and have really nothing to show for his wealth whatever. You go to his house, and you find nothing but a lot of shabby furniture. The only thing there which Seneca would have called wealth is perhaps his wife's jewels, which would not bring a few thousand dollars. You think his money must be in the bank, but you go there with him and find that all he has there is a page on the ledger bearing his name, with a few figures on it. The bank bills which you see lying about, and which look a little like money, are not only not money in the sense Seneca understood the term, but they do not represent over a third of what the bank owes to various people. You go to some safe-deposit vaults, thinking that it is perhaps there he keeps his valuables, but all you find is a mass of papers signed by Thomas Smith or John Jones, declaring that he is entitled to so many shares of some far-off bank, or that some railroad will pay him a certain sum some thirty years hence. In fact, looked at with Roman eyes, our millionaire seems to be possessed of little or nothing, and likely to be puzzled about his daily bread.

Now, this wonderful change in the character and incidents of property may be said to be the work of the last century, and it may be said to consist in the substitution of an agency wholly moral for an agency wholly material in the work of exchange and distribution. For the giving and receiving of gold and silver we have substituted neither more nor less than faith in the honesty and industry and capacity of our fellow-men. There is hardly one of us who does not literally live by faith. We lay up fortunes, marry, eat, drink, travel, and bequeath, almost without ever handling a cent; and the best reason which ninety-nine out of every hundred of us can give for feeling secure against want, or having the means of enjoyment or of charity, is not the possession of anything of real value, but his confidence that certain thousands of his fellow-creatures, whom he has never seen and never expects to see, scattered, it may be, over the civilized world, will keep their promises, and do their daily work with fidelity and efficiency. This faith is every year being made to carry a greater and greater load. The transactions which rest on it increase every year in magnitude and complexity. It has to extend itself every year over a larger portion of the earth's surface, and to include a greater variety of race and creed and custom. London and Paris and Berlin and Vienna now tremble when New York is alarmed. We have, in short, to believe every year in a greater and greater number of people, and to depend for our daily bread on the successful working of vast combinations, in which human character is, after all, the main element.

The consequence is that, when for any reason a shade of doubt comes over men's minds that the combination is not working, that the machine is at some point going to give way, that somebody is not playing his part fairly, the solid ground seems to shake under their feet, and we have some of the phenomena resulting from an earthquake, and among others blind terror. But to anyone who understands what this new social force, Credit, is, and the part it plays in human affairs, the wonder is, not that it gives way so seldom, but that it stands so firm; that these hundreds of millions of laborers, artisans, shopkeepers, merchants, bankers, and manufacturers hold so firmly from day to day the countless engagements into which they enter, and that each recurring year the result of the prodigious effort which is now put forth in the civilized world in the work of production should be distributed with so much accuracy and honesty, and, on the whole, with so much wise adjustment to the value of each man's contributions to civilization.

There is one fact, however, which throws around credit, as around so many others of the influences by which our lives are shaped, a frightful mystery. Its very strength helps to work ruin. The more we believe in our fellow-toilers, and the more they do to warrant our belief, the more we encourage them to work, the more we excite their hopefulness; and out of this hopefulness come "panics" and "crashes." Prosperity breeds credit, and credit stimulates enterprise, and enterprise embarks in labors which, about every ten years in England, and every twenty years in this country, it is found that the world is not ready to pay for. Panics have occurred in England in 1797, 1807, 1817, 1826, 1837, 1847, 1857, and there was very near being a very severe one in 1866. In this country we have had them in 1815, 1836, 1857, and 1877, and by panics we do not mean such local whirlwinds as have desolated Wall Street, but wide-spread commercial crises, affecting all branches of business. This periodicity is ascribed, and with much plausibility, to the fact that inasmuch as panics are the result of certain mental conditions, they recur as soon as the experience of the previous one has lost its influence, or, in other words, as often as a new generation comes into the management of affairs, which is about every ten years in the commercial world both in England and here. The fact that this country seems to be only half as liable to them as England, is perhaps due to the fact that the extent of our resources, and the greater ratio of increase of population make it much harder to overdo in the work of production here than in England, and to this must be added the greater strength of nerves produced by greater hopefulness. In spite of the enormous abundance of British capital and the rashness of the own-ers in making investments, there hangs over the London money market a timidity and doubtfulness about the future which is unknown on this side of the water, and which very slight accidents develop into distrust and terror.

Outside those who are actually engaged in a financial panic--such as brokers, bankers, merchants and manufacturers, who have loans to pay or receive, or accep-tances falling due, and who are therefore too busy and too sorely beset to moralize on it or look at it objectively, as the philosophers say--there is a large body of persons who are not immediately affected by it, such as professional men, owners of secure investments, persons in receipt of well-assured salaries, ministers, newspaper writ-ers, speculative economists, financiers, and farmers, to whom it is a source of secret enjoyment. They are obliged, out of sympathy with their neighbors, to look blue, and probably few of them are entirely exempt from the general anxiety about the future, but, nevertheless, they are on the whole rather gratified than otherwise by the thing's having happened. In the first place, all those persons who give their at-tention to the currency question are divided into two great schools--the paper men and the hard-money men; and every panic affords each of them what it considers a legitimate ground of triumph. The paper men say that the crisis is due to failure to issue more paper at the proper moment, and the hard-money men ascribe it to the irredeemability of what is already issued; and each side chuckles over the con-vulsion as a startling confirmation of its views, and goes about calling attention to it almost gleefully. There is a similar division on the banking question. Indeed the feud between the friends of free banking and restricted banking is fiercer than that between the two currency schools, and has raged longer, and every monetary crisis feeds the flame. It is maintained, on the one hand, that if banks were let alone by the state their issues would be proportioned to the exact wants of business; and, on the other, that if the state would only restrict them more rigidly business would be kept within proper limits, and all would go well. Each disputant draws from a panic about the same amount of support for his views, because in the great variety of circumstances which surround it there are always some which favor any theory of its origin. In one thing, however, both sets of observers are apt to agree thoroughly, and that is in believing the "thing will not blow over," and that "we are going to feel it for a long time." They have long foreseen it, and have only been surprised that it did not come sooner; and they lower their voices to a hoarse whisper while telling you this.

But there is no class of observers which extracts so much solid comfort from a panic as that large body of social philosophers who are hostile to luxury, and believe that the world is going to the dogs through self-indulgence. It may even be said that two-thirds of the community, or indeed all except the very few, hold this opinion with a greater or less degree of strength. The farmers hold it strongly with regard to the city people, the artisans with regard to merchants, bankers, brokers, and manufacturers, and among the latter nearly every man is inclined to it with regard to persons of more means than himself. Moreover, it would probably astonish us if we knew how large was the number of those who fancy that their more well-to-do neighbors, if they do not belong to the category of millionaires, are living beyond their means. Every man whose own means are small, or even moderate, finds himself rather hard put to it to make both ends meet, and is constantly harassed by desires which he is unable to gratify. When he sees others gratifying them, his self-love drives him often unconsciously into ascribing it to recklessness and improvidence. Very close people, too, who have a constitutional repugnance to spending money freely for any purpose, and especially for purposes of personal enjoyment, can hardly persuade themselves that other persons who do so, spend it honestly. And then behind these come the large army of lovers of simplicity and frugality on moral and religious grounds, who believe that material luxury contains a snare for the soul, and that true happiness and real virtue are not to be found in gilded saloons. They write to the newspapers denouncing the reluctance of young people to marry on small incomes, and urging girls to begin life as their mothers began it, and despise the silly chatter of those who think luxurious surroundings more important than the union of hearts.

The occurrence of a panic fills the breasts of all these with various degrees of rejoicing. They always take a very dark view of it, and laugh contemptuously at those who consider it a "Wall-Street flurry," or ascribe it to any vice in the currency or in the banking system. Extravagant living they believe to be at the bottom of it, and, like the hard-money men, they are only surprised that it has not come sooner, and they believe most firmly that it is going to effect a sort of social revolution, and bring the world more nearly to their own ideal of what it ought to be. The amount of "rottenness" which they expect it to reveal is always enormous, and they look forward to the exposure and the general coming-down of their guilty neighbors to "the hard pan" with the keenest relish. They have long, for instance, been unable to imagine where the multitude of people who live in brown-stone houses get the money to keep them. There was something wrong about it, they felt satisfied, though they could not tell what, and when the panic comes they half fancy that the murder will out, and that there will be a great migration of fraudulent bankrupts from Fifth Avenue and its neighborhood into tenement-houses on the East and North Rivers. How Mrs. Smith, too, dressed as she did, and where Smith got the money to take her to Sharon every summer, and how Jones managed to entertain as he was doing, have often been puzzling problems, which "the crash" in the money market is at last going to solve. It is also highly gratifying to those who consider yachting a senseless amusement to reflect that the panic will probably diminish the number of yachts, and they even flatter themselves that it may stop yachting in future, and reduce the general style of living among rich young men. "We shall now," they say, "have fewer fast horses, and less champagne, and less gaudy furniture, and more honest, hard work, and plain, wholesome food." They accordingly rejoice in the panic as a means adopted by Providence to bring a gluttonous and ungodly generation to its senses, and lead it back to that state of things which is known, as "republican simplicity."

The curious thing about this expectation is that it has survived innumerable disappointments without apparently losing any of its vigor. It was strong after 1837, and strong after 1857, and stronger than ever after 1861. The war was surely, people

said, to bring back the golden age, when all the men were prudent, sober, and industrious, and all the women simple, modest, and homekeeping. The war did nothing of the kind. In fact, it left us more extravagant and lavish and self-indulgent
than ever; yet the ancient and tough belief in the purifying influence of a stringent
money market still lasts, and is at this moment cropping out in the moral department of a thousand newspapers.

The belief belongs to what may be called the cataclysmal theory of progress,
which improves the world by sudden starts, and clings so fondly to liquor-laws,
and has profound faith in specific remedies for moral and political diseases. What
commercial panics and great national misfortunes do not do, particular bits of legislation are sure to do. You put something in the Constitution, or forbid something,
or lose a battle, or have a "shrinkage of values," or have a cholera season, and forth-
with the community turns over a new leaf, and becomes moral, economical, and
sober-minded. We doubt whether this theory will ever die out, however much
philosophers may preach against it, or however often facts may refute it, because it
gratifies, or promises to gratify, one of the deepest longings of the human heart--the
desire which each man feels to have a great deal of history crowded into his own
little day. None of us can bear to quit the scene without witnessing the solution
of the problems by which his own life has been vexed or over which he has long
labored. Indeed a great many men would find it impossible to work with any zeal
to bring about results which would probably not be witnessed until they had been
centuries in the tomb.

We accordingly find that the most eager reformers are apt to be those who look
for the triumph of virtue by the close of the current year. Of all dreams of eager
reformers, however, there is probably none more substantial than that which looks
for a restoration of that vague thing called "simplicity of manners." Simplicity and
economy are, of course, relative terms. The luxurious gentleman in the fourteenth
century lived in a way which the well-to-do artisan in our own time would not tol-
erate; and when we undertake to carry people back to ancient ways of living we find
that there is hardly a point short of barbarism at which we can consistently stop. A
country in which money is easily made and abounds, will be one in which money
will always be freely spent, and in which personal comfort and even display will occupy men's and women's thoughts a great deal. We can no more prevent this than

we can prevent the growth of wealth itself; and our duty is, instead of wasting our breath in denouncing extravagance, or hailing panics as purging fires, to do what in us lies to give rich people more taste, more conscience, more sense of responsibility for curable ills, and a keener relish of the higher forms of pleasure. Extravagance--or, in other words, the waste of money on sensual enjoyment, the production of hideous furniture or jewelry, or of barbarous display--has to be checked not by the preaching of poor people, but by the rich man's own superiority to these things, and his own repugnance for them. This repugnance can only be inspired by education, whether that of school and college, or that of a refined and cultivated social atmosphere. Much would be done in this direction if public opinion exacted of the owners of large fortunes that they should give their sons the best education the country affords; or, in other words, send them to college, instead of setting them up in the dry-goods business or the grocery business. A man who has made a large fortune in honest trade or industry has not contributed his share to moral and intellectual interests by merely making donations. It is his duty, also, if he leaves children behind him, to see to it, as far as he can, that they are men who will be an addition to the general culture and taste of the nation, and who will stimulate its nobler ambition, raise its intellectual standard, quicken its love of excellence in all fields, and deepen its faith in the value of things not seen.

THE ODIUM PHILOLOGICUM

Our readers and those of **The Galaxy** are familiar with the controversy between Dr. Fitzedward Hall and Mr. Grant White (November, 1873). When one comes to inquire what it was all about, and why Mr. White was led to consider Dr. Hall a "yahoo of literature," and "a man born without a sense of decency," one finds himself engaged in an investigation of great difficulty, but of considerable interest. The controversy between these two gentlemen by no means brings up the problem for the first time. That verbal criticism, such as Mr. White has been producing for some time back, is sure to end, sooner or later, in one or more savage quarrels, is one of the most familiar facts of the literary life of our day. Indeed, so far as our observation has gone, the rule has no exceptions. Whenever we see a gentleman, no matter how great his accomplishments or sweet his temper, announcing that he is about to write articles or deliver lectures on "Words and their Uses," or on the "English of Every-day Life," or on "Familiar Faults of Conversation," or "Newspaper English," or any cognate theme, we feel all but certain that we shall soon see him engaged in an encounter with another laborer in the same field, in which all dignity will be laid aside, and in which, figuratively speaking, clothes, hair, and features will suffer terribly, and out of which, unless he is very lucky, he will issue with the gravest imputations resting on his character in every relation of life.

Now why is it that attempts to get one's fellow-men to talk correctly, to frame their sentences in accordance with good usage, and take their words from the best authors, have this tendency to arouse some of the worst passions of our nature, and predispose even eminent philologists--men of dainty language, and soft manners, and lofty aims--to assail each other in the rough vernacular of the fish-market and the forecastle? A careless observer will be apt to say that it is an ordinary result of disputation; that when men differ or argue on any subject they are apt to get angry and indulge in "personalities." But this is not true. Lawyers, for instance, live by controversy, and their controversies touch interests of the gravest and most deli-cate character--such as fortune and reputation; and yet the spectacle of two lawyers abusing each other in cold blood, in print, is almost unknown. Currency and bank-ing are, at certain seasons, subjects of absorbing interest, and, for the last seventy years, the discussions over them have been numerous and voluminous almost be-yond example, and yet we remember no case in which a bullionist called a paper-money man bad names, or in which a friend of free banking accused a restrictionist of defrauding the poor or defacing tombstones. Politics, too, home and foreign, is a fertile source of difference of opinion; and yet gross abuse, on paper, of each other, by political disputants, discussing abstract questions having no present relation to power or pay, are very rare indeed.

It seems, at first blush, as if an examination of the well-known ***odium theologi-cum***, or the traditional bitterness which has been apt to characterize controversies about points of doctrine, from the Middle Ages down to a period within our own memory, would throw some light on the matter. But a little consideration will show that there are special causes for the rancor of theologians for which word-criticism has no parallel. The ***odium theologicum*** was the natural and inevitable result of the general belief that the holding of certain opinions was necessary to salvation, and that the formation of opinions could be wholly regulated by the will. This belief, pushed to its extreme limits and embodied in legislation, led to the burning of heretics in nearly all Christian countries. When B's failure to adopt A's conclusions was by A regarded as a sign of depravity of nature which, would lead to B's damnation, nothing was more natural than that when they came into collision in pamphlets or sermons they should have attributed to each other the worst motives. A man who was deliberately getting himself ready for perdition was not a person to whom anybody owed courtesy or consideration, or whose arguments, being probably supplied by Satan, deserved respectful examination. We accordingly find that as the list of "essential" opinions has become shortened, and as doubts as to men's responsibility for their opinions have made their way from the world into the church, theological controversy has lost its acrimony and indeed has almost ceased. No theologian of high standing or character now permits himself to show bad temper in a doctrinal or hermeneutical discussion, and a large and increasing proportion of theologians acknowledge that the road to heaven is so hard for us all that the less quarrelling and jostling there is in it, the better for everybody.

Nor does the ***odium scientificum***, of which we have now happily but occasional manifestations, furnish us with any suggestions. Controversy between scientific men begins to be bitter and frequent, as the field of investigation grows wider and the investigation itself grows deeper. But then this is easily accounted for. All scientific men of the first rank are engaged in original research--that is, in attempts to discover laws and phenomena previously unknown. The workers in all departments are very numerous, and are scattered over various countries, and as one discovery, however slight, is very apt to help in some degree in the making of another, scientific men are constantly exposed to having their claims to originality contested, either as regards priority in point of time or as regards completeness. Consequently, they may be said to stand in delicate relations to each other, and are more than usually sensitive about the recognition of their achievements by their brethren--a state of things which, while it cultivates a very nice sense of honor, leads occasionally to encounters in which free-will seems for the moment to get the better of law. The differences of the scientific world, too, are complicated by the theological bearing of a good deal of scientific discovery and discussion, and many a scientific man finds himself either compelled to defend himself against theologians, or to aid theologians in bringing an erring brother to reason.

The true source of the ***odium philologicum*** is, we think, to be found in the fact that a man's speech is apt to be, or to be considered, an indication of the manner in which he has been bred, and of the character of the company he keeps. Criticism of his mode of using words, or his pronunciation, or the manner in which he compounds his sentences, almost inevitably takes the character of an attack on his birth, parentage, education, and social position; or, in other words, on everything which he feels most sensitive about or holds most dear. If you say that his pronunciation is bad, or that his language is slangy or ill-chosen, you insinuate that when he lived at home with his papa and mamma he was surrounded by bad models, or, in plain English, that his parents were vulgar or ignorant people; when you say that he writes bad grammar, or is guilty of glaring solecisms, or displays want of etymological knowledge, you insinuate that his education was neglected, or that he has not associated with correct speakers. Usually, too, you do all this in the most provoking way by selecting passages from his writings on which he probably prided himself, and separating them totally from the thought of which he was full when he produced them, and then examining them mechanically, as if they were algebraic signs, which he used without knowing what they meant or where they would bring him out. Nobody stands this process very long with equanimity, because nobody can be subjected to it without being presented to the public somewhat in the light of an ignorant, careless, and pretentious donkey. Nor will it do to cite your examples from deceased authors. You cannot do so without assailing some form of expression which an eager, listening enemy is himself in the habit of using, and is waiting for you to take up, and through which he hopes to bring you to shame.

No man, moreover, can perform the process without taking on airs which rouse his victim to madness, because he assumes a position not only of grammatical, but, as we have said, of social superiority. He says plainly enough, no matter how polite or scientific he may try to seem, "I was better born and bred than you, and acquired these correct turns of expression, of which you know nothing, from cultivated relatives;" or, "I live in cultivated circles, and am consequently familiar with the best usage, which you, poor fellow! are not. I am therefore able to decide this matter without argument or citations, and your best course is to take my corrections in silence or with thankfulness." It is easy to understand how all interest in orthography, etymology, syntax, and prosody speedily disappears in a controversy of this sort, and how the disputants begin to burn with mutual dislike, and how each longs to inflict pain and anguish on his opponent, and make him, no matter by what means, an object of popular pity and contempt, and make his parts of speech odious and ridiculous. The influence of all good men ought to be directed either to repressing verbal criticism, or restricting indulgence in it to the family circle or to schools and colleges.

PROFESSOR HUXLEY'S LECTURES

Biologist like Professor Huxley have, as popular lecturers, the advantage over scientific men in other fields, of occupying themselves with what is to ninety-nine men and women out of a hundred the most momentous of all problems--the manner in which life on this globe began, and in which men and other animals came to be what they are. The doctrine of evolution as a solution of these problems, or of one of them, derives additional interest from the fact that in many minds it runs counter to ideas which a very large proportion of the population above the age of thirty imbibed with the earliest and most impressive portion of their education. Down to 1850 the bulk of intelligent men and women believed that the world, and all that is therein, originated in the precise manner described in the first chapter of Genesis, and about six thousand years ago. Most of the adaptations, or attempts at adaptation, of what is called the Mosaic account of the creation, of the chronological theories of the geologists and evolutionists by theologians and Biblical scholars have been made within that period, and it may be safely said that it is only within ten or fifteen years that any clear knowledge of the "conflict between science and religion" has reached that portion of the people who take a lively or, indeed, any interest, in religious matters. It would not, in fact, be rash to say that little or nothing is known about this conflict to this hour among the great body of Methodists or Catholics, or the evangelical portion of other denominations, and that their religious outlook is little, if at all, affected by it. One would never detect, for instance, in Mr. Moody's preaching, any indication that he had ever heard of any such conflict, or that the doctrines of the orthodox Protestant Church had undergone any sensible modification within a hundred years. Professor Huxley and men like him, therefore, make their appearance now not simply as manipulators of a most interesting subject, but as disturbers of beliefs which are widely spread, deeply rooted, and surrounded by the tenderest and most sacred associations of human existence.

That under such circumstances he has met with so little opposition is, on the whole, rather surprising. As far as our observation has gone, no strong hostility whatever to himself or his teachings has been shown, except in one or two instances, by either the clergy or the religious press. Indeed, ministers formed a very prominent and attentive portion of his audience at the recent lectures at Chickering Hall. But it has been made very apparent by the articles and letters which these lectures have called out in the newspapers that the religious public has hardly understood him. The collision between the theologians and the scientific men has been very slight among us; and, indeed, the waves of the controversy hardly reached this country until the storm had passed away in Europe, so that it is difficult for Americans to appreciate the combative tone of Mr. Huxley's oratory. Of this difficulty the effect of his substitution of Milton for Moses as the historian of the creation, on the night of his first lecture, has furnished an amusing illustration. The audience, or at least that portion of it which was gifted with any sense of humor, saw the joke and laughed over it heartily. It was simply a telling rhetorical device, intended to point a sarcasm directed against the biblical commentators who have been trying to extract the doctrines of evolution from the first chapter of Genesis. But many of the newspapers all over the country took it up seriously, and the professor must, if he saw them, have enjoyed mightily the various letters and articles which have endeavored in solemn earnest to show that Milton was not justly entitled to the rank of a scientific expositor, and that it was a cowardly thing in the lecturer to attack Moses over Milton's shoulders. Whenever Professor Huxley enters on the defence of his science, as distinguished from the exposition of it, there are traces in his language of the ***gaudium certaminis*** which has found expression in so many hard-fought fields in his own country, and which has made him perhaps the most formidable antagonist, in so far as dialectics go, that the transcendental philosophers have ever encountered. He is, ***par excellence***, a fighting man, but certainly his pugnacity diminishes neither his worth nor his capacity.

In many of the comments which his lectures have called out in the newspapers one meets every now and then with a curious failure to comprehend the position which an average non-scientific man occupies in such a conflict as in now going on over the doctrines of evolution. Professor Huxley was very careful not to repeat the error which delivered Professor Tyndall into the hands of the enemy at Belfast. He expressed no opinion as to the nature of the causal force which called the world into existence. He did not profess to know anything about the sources of life. He consequently did not once place himself on the level of the theologian or the unscientific spectator. What he undertook to do and did was to present to the audience some specimens of the evidence by which evolutionists have been led to the conclusion that their theory is correct. Now, the mistake which a good many newspaper writers--some of them ministers--have made in passing judgment on the lectures lies in their supposing that this evidence must be weak and incomplete because *they* have not been convinced. There is probably no more widely diffused fallacy, or one which works more mischief in all walks of life, than the notion that it is only those whose business it is to persuade who need to be trained in the art of proof, and that those who are to be persuaded need no process of preparation at all.

The fact is that skill in reasoning is as necessary on the one side as the other. He cannot be fully and rightly convinced who does not himself know how to convince, and no man is competent to judge in the last resort of the force of an argument who is not on something like an equality of knowledge and dialectical skill with the person using it. This is true in all fields of discussion; it is pre-eminently true in scientific fields. Of course, therefore, the real public of the scientific man--the public which settles finally whether he has made out his case--is a small one. Outside of it there is another and larger one on which his reasoning may act with irresistible force; but just as the fact that it does so act does not prove that his hypothesis is true, so also the fact that it has failed to convince proves nothing against its soundness. In other words, a man's occupying the position of a listener does not necessarily clothe him with the attributes of a judge, and there may be as much folly and impertinence in his going about saying, "I do not agree with Huxley; he has not satisfied me; he will have to produce more proof than that before I believe in evolution," as in going about saying, "I know as much about evolution as Huxley and could give as good a lecture on it as he any day." And yet a good many people are guilty of the one who would blush at the mere thought of the other.

Another fertile source of confusion in this and similar controversies is the habit which transcendentalists, theological and other, have of using the term "truth" in two different senses, the scientific sense and the religious or spiritual sense. The scientific man only uses it in one. Truth to him is something capable of demonstration by some one of the canons of induction. He knows nothing of any truth which cannot be proved. The religious man, on the other hand, and especially the minister, has been bred in the application of the term to facts of an entirely different order-- that is, to emotions produced by certain beliefs which he cannot justify by any arguments, and about which to him no argument is necessary. These are the "spiritual truths" which are said to be perceptible often to the simple-minded and unlearned, though hidden from the wise and prudent. Now there is no decently educated religious man who does not perceive the distinction between these two kinds of truths, and few who do not think they keep this distinction in mind when passing upon the great problems of the origin and growth of the universe. But, as a matter of fact, we see the distinction ignored every day. People go to scientific lectures and read scientific books with their heads filled with spiritual truths, which have come they know not whence, and which give them infinite comfort in all the trying passages of life, and in view of this comfort must, they think, connect them by invisible lines of communication with the great Secret of the Universe, toward which philosophers try to make their way by visible lines. When, then, they find that the scientific man's induction makes no impression on this other truth, and that he cannot dislodge any theory of the growth or government of the world which has become firmly imbedded in it, they are apt to conclude that there is something faulty in his methods, or rash and presumptuous in his conclusions. But there is only one course for the leaders of religious thought to follow in order to prevent the disastrous confusion which comes of the sudden and complete break-down of the moral standards and sanctions by which the mass of mankind live, and that is to put an end at once, and gracefully, to the theory that the spiritual truth which brings the peace which passeth understanding has any necessary connection with any theory of the physical universe, or can be used to refute it or used as a substitute for it, or is dependent on the authenticity or interpretation of any book. They must not flatter themselves because a scientific man here and there doubts or gainsays, or because some learned theologian is still unconvinced, or because the mental habits of which faith is born seem to hold their ground or show signs of revival, that the philosophy of which Huxley is a master is not slowly but surely gaining ground. The proofs may not yet be complete, but they grow day by day; some of the elder scientific men may scout, but no young ones are appearing to take their places and preach their creed. The tide seems sometimes to ebb from month to month, but it rises from year to year. The true course of spiritually minded men under these circumstances is to separate their faith from all theories of the precise manner in which the world originated, or of the length of time it has lasted, as matters, for their purposes, of little or no moment. The secret springs of hope and courage from which each of us draws strength in the great crises of existence would flow all the same whether life appeared on the planet ten million or ten thousand years ago, and whether the present forms of life were the product of one day or of many ages. And we doubt very much whether anyone has ever listened in a candid and dispassionate frame of mind to the evolutionist's history of the globe without finding that it had deepened for him the mystery of the universe, and magnified the Power which stands behind it.

Not the least interesting feature in the discussion about the theory of evolution is the prominent part taken in it by clergymen of various denominations. There is hardly one of them who, since Huxley's lectures, has not preached a sermon bearing on the matter in some way, and several have made it the topic of special articles or lectures. In fact, we do not think we exaggerate when we say that three-fourths of all that has been recently said or written about the hypothesis in this country has been said or written by ministers. There is no denying that the theory, if true, does, in appearance at least, militate against the account of the creation given in the first chapter of Genesis, or, in other words, against the view of the origin of life on the globe which has been held by the Christian world for seventeen centuries. It would, therefore, be by no means surprising that ministers should meet it, either by showing that the Mosaic account of the creation was really inspired--was, in short, the account given by the Creator himself--or that the modern interpretations of it were incorrect, and that it was really, when perfectly understood, easily reconciled with the conclusions reached of late years by geologists and biologists. This is the way in which a great many ministers have hitherto met the evolutionists, and for this sort of work they are undoubtedly fitted by education and experience. If it can be done by anyone, they are the men to do it. If it be maintained that the biblical account is literally true, they are more familiar than any other class of men with the evidence and arguments accumulated by the Church in favor of the inspiration of the Scriptures; or if, on the other hand, it be desired to reconcile the Bible with evolution, they are more familiar than any other class of men with the exegetical process by which this reconciliation can be effected. They are specially trained in ecclesiastical history and tradition, in Greek and Hebrew religious literature, and in the methods of interpretation which have been for ages in use among theologians.

Of late, however, they have shown a decided inclination to abandon the purely ecclesiastical approach to the controversy altogether, and this is especially remarkable in the discussion now pending over Huxley. They do not seek to defend the biblical account of the creation, or to reconcile it with the theory of the evolutionists. Far from it, they have come down, in most of the recent cases, into the scientific arena, and are meeting the men of science with their own weapons. They tell Huxley and Darwin and Tyndall that their evidence is imperfect, and their reasoning from it faulty. Noticing their activity in this new field, and the marked contrast which this activity presents to the modesty or indifference of the other professions--the lawyers and doctors, for instance, who on general grounds have fully as much reason to be interested in evolution as the ministers, and have hitherto been at least as well fitted to discuss it--we asked ourselves whether it was possible that, without our knowledge, any change had of late years been made in the curriculum of the divinity schools or theological seminaries with the view of fitting ministers to take a prominent part in the solution of the increasingly important and startling problems raised by physical science. In order to satisfy ourselves, we lately turned over the catalogues of all the principal divinity schools in the country, to see if any chairs of natural science had been established, or if candidates for the ministry had to undergo any compulsory instruction in geology or physics, or the higher mathematics, or biology, or palaeontology, or astronomy, or had to become versed in the methods of scientific investigation in the laboratory or in the dissecting-room, or were subjected to any unusually severe discipline in the use of the inductive process. Not much to our surprise, we found nothing of the kind. We found that, to all appearance, not even the smallest smattering of natural science in any of its branches is considered necessary to a minister's education; no astronomy, no chemistry, no biology, no geology, no higher mathematics, no comparative anatomy, and nothing severe in logic. In fact, of special preparation for the discussion of such a theme as the origin of life on the earth, there does not appear to be in the ordinary course of our divinity schools any trace.

We then said to ourselves, But ministers are modest, truthful men; they would not knowingly pass themselves off as competent on a subject with which they were unfitted to deal. They are no less candid and self-distrustful, for instance, than lawyers and doctors, and a lawyer or doctor who ventured to tackle a professed scientist on a scientific subject to which he had given no systematic study would be laughed at by his professional brethren, and would suffer from it even in his professional reputation, as it would be taken to indicate a dangerous want of self-knowledge. Perhaps, then, the training given in the divinity schools, though it does not touch special fields of science, is such as to prepare the mind for the work of induction by some course of intellectual gymnastics. Perhaps, though it does not familiarize a man with the facts of geology and biology and astronomy, it so disciplines him in the work of collecting and arranging facts of any kind, and reasoning from them, that he will be a master in the art of proof, and that, in short, though he may not have a scientific man's knowledge, he will have his mental habits.

But we found this second supposition as far from the truth as the first one was. Moreover, the mental constitution of the young men who choose the ministry as a profession is not apt to be of a kind well fitted for scientific investigation. Reverence is one of their prominent characteristics, and reverence predisposes them to accept things on authority. They are inclined to seek truth rather as a means of repose than for its own sake, and to fancy that it is associated closely with spiritual comfort, and that they have secured the truth when they feel the comfort. Though, last not least, they enter the seminary with a strong bias in favor of one particular theory of the origin of life and of the history of the race, and their subsequent studies are marked out and pursued with the set purpose of strengthening this bias and of qualifying them to defend it and spread it, and of associating in their minds the doubt or rejection of it with moral evil. The consequence is that they go forth, trained not as investigators or inquirers, but as advocates, charged with the defence against all comers of a view of the universe which they have accepted ready-made from teachers. A worse preparation for scientific pursuits of any kind can hardly be imagined. The slightest trace of such a state of mind in a scientific man--that is, of a disposition to believe a thing on grounds of feeling or interest, or with reference to practical consequences, or to jump over gaps in proof in order to reach pleasant conclusions--discredits him with his fellows, and throws doubt on his statements.

We are not condemning this state of mind for all purposes. Indeed, we think the wide-spread prevalence of the philosophic way of looking at things would be in many respects a great misfortune for the race, and we acknowledge that a rigidly trained philosopher would be unfit for most of a minister's functions; but we have only to describe a minister's education in order to show his exceeding unreadiness for contentions such as some of his brethren are carrying on with geologists and physicists and biologists. In fact, there is no educated calling whose members are not, on the whole, better equipped for fighting in scientific fields over the hypothesis of evolution. Our surprise at seeing lawyers and doctors engaged in it would be very much less justifiable, for a portion at least of the training received in these professions is of a scientific cast, and concerns the selection and classification of facts, while a clergyman's is almost wholly devoted to the study of the opinions and sayings of other men. In truth, theology, properly so called, is a collection of opinions. Nor do these objections to a clergyman's mingling in scientific disputes arise out of his belief about the origin and government of the world *per se*, because one does not think of making them to trained religious philosophers; for instance, to Principal Dawson or Mr. St. George Mivart. Some may think or say that the religious prepossessions of these gentlemen lessen the weight of their opinions on a certain class of scientific questions, but no one would question their right to share in scientific discussions.

CIRCUMSTANTIAL EVIDENCE

Some of the letters from clergymen which have been called out by our article on the part recently taken by them in scientific discussion maintain that, although ministers may not be familiar with the facts of science, many of them are fully competent to weigh the arguments founded on these facts put forward by scientific men, and decide whether they have proved their case or not; or, in other words, that we were mistaken in saying that the theological seminaries did not afford severe training in the use of the inductive process, and that it could not be used effectively without knowledge of the matters on which it was used. More than one of these letters points, in support of this view, to the answer of the Rev. Dr. Taylor, of this city, to Professor Huxley's lectures, published some weeks ago in the *Tribune*, and we believe the *Tribune* presented the author to the public as "a trained logician."

We have accordingly turned to Dr. Taylor's letter and given it a much more attentive reading than we confess we gave it when it first appeared, for the purpose of seeing whether it was really true that ministers were such dexterous and highly taught dialecticians that they could overthrow a scientific man, even on a subject of which they knew little or nothing--whether, in short, they could really treat the question of evolution algebraically, and, by the mere aid of signs of the meaning of which they were ignorant, put the Huxleys and Darwins to confusion. For Dr. Taylor opens in this way:

> "Let it be understood, then, that I have no fault to find with Mr. Huxley as a discoverer of facts or as an exponent of comparative anatomy. In both of these respects he is beyond all praise of mine, and I am ready to sit at his feet; but when he begins to reason from the facts which he sets forth, then, like every other reasoner, he is amenable to the laws of argumentation, and his conclusions are to be tested by the relation which they bear to the premises which he has advanced, and by the proof which he furnishes for the premises themselves."

We pass over, as of no consequence for our present purpose, the various exceptions which he then takes to Huxley's arrangement of his lectures, to the tone of his exceptions, and to his mode of referring to the biblical hypothesis, and come to what he has to say of Huxley's evidence, which he truly calls "circumstantial evidence." The first thing he does is to define circumstantial evidence; but here, at the very outset, we have been surprised to find a logician who conceives himself capable of overhauling the argumentation of the masters of science, going to a lawyer to get "a statement of the principles which regulate the value of circumstantial evidence." This is a matter which lay logicians usually have at their fingers' ends, and we have never known one yet who would not be puzzled by a suggestion that he should do as Dr. Taylor did--go to a "distinguished legal friend" for information as to the conditions of this kind of proof. For, as we have more than once pointed out, lawyers, as such, have no special skill or training in the use of circumstantial evidence as scientific men know it--that is, as evidence which derives all its force from the laws of the human mind. The circumstantial evidence with which lawyers, *qua* lawyers, are familiar under our system of jurisprudence is an artificial thing created by legislation or custom, with the object of preventing the minds of the jury-- presumably a body of untrained and unlearned men--from being confused or led astray. Moreover, they are only familiar with its use in one very narrow field--human conduct under one set of social conditions. For example, a lawyer might be a very good judge of circumstantial evidence in America, and a very poor one in India or China; might have a keen eye for the probable or improbable in a New England village, and none at all in a Prussian barrack.

A familiar illustration of the restrictions on his experience of it is to be found in the rule which compels the calling of "experts" when there is a question as to any point of science or art. "The words science or art," says Mr. Fitzjames Stephen, "include all subjects on which a *course of special study or experience is necessary to the formation of an opinion*," and the opinion of such an expert is a "relevant fact." So that Dr. Taylor's "distinguished legal friend," if a good lawyer, would not, in spite of his proficiency in circumstantial evidence, undertake to dispute with Professor Huxley about the relation of the anchitherium, hipparion, and horse; and if Dr. Taylor offered himself for examination on such a point he would be laughed out of court. In none of our courts is the presentation allowed of *all* the circumstances which strengthen or weaken a probability.

A lawyer, therefore, though he might not be as ill fitted for a scientific discussion as a minister, is, *as such*, hardly more of an authority on the force and limits of that portion of scientific proof which is drawn from simple observation. Dr. Taylor's consulting one as a final authority as to the very nature of the argument on which he was himself about to sit in judgment is at the outset a suspicious incident. The definition of circumstantial evidence which he got from his legal friend was this:

"The process of proof by circumstantial evidence consists in reasoning from such facts as are known or proved, and thence establishing such as are conjectured to exist. The process is fatally vicious, first, if any material circumstance from which we seek to deduce the conclusion depends itself on conjecture; and, second, if the known facts are not such as to exclude to a reasonable degree of certainty every other hypothesis."

"Now, tried by these two tests," says Dr. Taylor, "the professor's argument was a failure." Taking this definition as it stands, however, we think it will not be difficult to show that Dr. Taylor is not competent to apply the tests, or to say whether the professor's argument is a failure or not.

It is hardly necessary to say that all the evidence in our possession or attainable, with regard to the history of the earth and of animal and vegetable life on its surface, is circumstantial evidence. The sciences of geology, palaeontology, and, to a certain extent, biology are sciences of observation, and but few of their conclusions can be reached or tested by experimentation. They are the result of a collection of facts, observed in various places, at various times, and by various persons, and variously related to other facts; and the collection of these facts, and the arrangement of them, and the formation of a judgment as to their value both positive and relative, form the greater portion of the work of a scientific man in these fields. Professor Huxley's argument, which Dr. Taylor disposes of so summarily, consists of a series of inferences from facts so collected and arranged. They are the things "known or proved," on which, as his legal friend truly says, the reasoning in the process of proof by circumstantial evidence must rest.

Now, Dr. Taylor, by his own confession, is no authority in either geology, biology, or palaeontology. He has neither collected, observed, nor experimented in these fields. He does not know how many facts have been discovered in them, or what bearing they have on other facts in other fields. Therefore, he is entirely unable to say whether Huxley is arguing from things "known or proved" or not. Moreover, he does not, for similar reasons, know whether Huxley's process has been "fatally vitiated" by the dependence of any "material circumstance" on conjecture, or by the insufficiency of the "known facts" to exclude every other hypothesis; for, first, he does not know what is in geological, biological, or palaeontological induction a "material circumstance"--nor does any man know except by prolonged study and observation--and, second, he does not know whether "the known or proved facts" are sufficient to exclude every other hypothesis, because he neither knows what facts are known nor what is the probative force of such as are known. We can, however, make Dr. Taylor's position still clearer by a homely illustration. A wild Indian will, owing to prolonged observation and great acuteness of the senses, tell by a simple inspection of grass or leaf-covered ground, on which a scholar will perceive nothing unusual whatever, that a man has recently passed over it. He will tell whether he was walking or running, whether he carried a burden, whether he was young or old, and how long ago and what hour of the day he went by. He reaches all his conclusions by circumstantial evidence of precisely the same character as that used by the geologist, though he knows nothing about the formal logic or the process of induction. Now, what Dr. Taylor would have us believe is that he can come out of his study and pass judgment on the Indian's reasoning without being able to see one of the "known facts" on which the reasoning rests, or appreciate in any degree which of them is material to the conclusion and which is not, or even to conjecture whether, taken together, they exclude the hypothesis that it was not a man but a cow or a dog which passed over the ground, and not to-day but yesterday that the marks were made.

Dr. Taylor further on makes a display of this inability to appreciate the logical value of scientific facts by asking: "Where is the evidence, scientific or other, that there was evolution? We see these fossils (those of the horse). Huxley *says* they are as they are because the higher evolved itself out of the lower; we *say* they are as they are because God created them in series." To recur to the former illustration, it is as if the Indian should show Dr. Taylor the marks on which he relied in his induction, and the doctor should calmly reply: "I see the marks; you *say* they were made by a man's foot in walking; I, who have never given any attention to the subject, and have never been in the woods before, *say* they were made by the rain." The fact is that if there were any weight whatever in this kind of talk--if no equality of knowledge were necessary between two disputants--it would enable an ignorant field-hand to sweep away in one sentence the whole science of geology and palaeontology, and even astronomy, and to dispose of every conclusion on any subject drawn from a skilled and experienced balancing of probabilities, or nice mathematical calculation, by simply saying that he was not satisfied with the proofs.

Dr. Taylor's reasons for believing that the appearance of fossil horses with a diminishing number of toes is caused by the creation at separate periods of a four-, a three-, a two-, and a one-toed horse are, he says, "personal, philosophical, historical," and he opposes them with the utmost apparent sincerity to Huxley's assertion that "there can be no scientific evidence" of such creation. The "personal reason" for believing in successive creations of sets of horses with a varying number of toes can, of course, only be the reason so often urged in ball-room disputation--that "I *feel* it must be so;" the "philosophic reason" can only be the one with which those who have frequented the society of metaphysicians are very familiar, namely, a deduction from some eminent speculator's opinion about the nature of the Supreme Being, the conclusion being apparently that if the Creator wished to diminish the number of a horse's toes, it would not do for him to let one drop into disuse and so gradually disappear, but he would have to make a new horse, on a new design. What Dr. Taylor means by the "historical reason" we can only conjecture from his saying that it is of the same order as his historical reason for believing "that the Bible is the Word of God." The historical reason for this, we presume, is that there are various literary and traditional proofs that the Old Testament was held to be the Word of God by the Jewish nation at a very early period, and was by them transmitted as such to the modern Christian world, and that many of the prophecies contained in it have received partial or a complete fulfilment. But how by a process of this kind, partly literary and partly conjectural, and attended by great difficulties at every step, he would reach a fact of *prehistoric times* of so much gravity as creation in series, we think it would puzzle Dr. Taylor to explain. Indeed, the mere production in a controversy of this nature of these vague fancies, half pious, half poetical, conjured up in most cases as a help to mental peace, by a leading minister in the character of a logician, is a very remarkable proof of the extent of those defects in clerical education to which we recently called attention.

TYNDALL AND THE THEOLOGIANS

The recent address delivered by Professor Tyndall before the British Association at Belfast, in which he "confessed" that he "prolonged the vision backward across the boundary of experimental evidence, and discerned in matter the promise and potency of every quality and form of life," produced one by no means very surprising result. Dr. Watts, a professor of theology in the Presbyterian College in that city, was led by it to offer to read before the Biological Section of the Association a paper containing a plan of his own for the establishment of "peace and co-operation between science and religion." The paper was, as might have been expected, declined. The author then read it before a large body of religious people, who apparently liked it, and they passed him a vote of thanks. The whole religious world, indeed, is greatly excited against both Tyndall and Huxley for their performances on this occasion, and papers by no means in sympathy with the religious world--the **Pall Mall Gazette**, for instance--are very severe on them for having "recourse to a style of oratory and disquisition more appropriate to the chapel than the lecture-room," or, in other words, for using the meetings of the Association for a sort of propagandism not much superior in method to that of theological missionaries, and thus challenging the theologians to a conflict which may make it necessary, in the interest of fair play, to add a theological section to the Association. Of course, when Professor Tyndall passed "beyond the boundary of experimental evidence," and began to see with his "mind's eye" instead of with the microscope and telescope, he got into a region in which the theologian is not only more at home than he, but which theology claims as its exclusive domain, and in which ministers look on physicists as intruders.

But then, Dr. Watts's "plea for peace and co-operation between science and religion" is one of many signs that theologians are, in spite of all that has as yet been said, hardly alive to the exact nature of the attitude they occupy toward science. They evidently look upon scientific men as they look on a hostile school of theologians--as the Princeton men look on the Yale men, for instance, or the New looked on the Old School Presbyterians, or the Calvinists on the Arminians--that is, as persons having a common standard of orthodoxy, but differing somewhat in their method of applying it, and who may, therefore, be induced from considerations of expediency to suppress all outward marks of divergence and work together harmoniously for the common end. All schools of theology seek the glory of God and salvation of souls, and, this being the case, differences on points of doctrine do seem trifling and capable of being put aside.

It is this way of regarding the matter which has led Dr. Watts to propose an alliance between religion and science, and which produces the arguments one sometimes sees in defence of Christianity against Positivism, drawn from a consideration of the services which Christianity has rendered to the race, and of the gloomy and desolate condition in which its disappearance would leave the world. Tyndall and Huxley do not, however, occupy the position of religious prophets or fathers. They preside over no church or other organization. They have no power or authority to draft any creed or articles which will bind anybody else, or which would have any claims on anybody's reverence or adhesion. No person, in short, is authorized to bring science into an alliance with religion or with anything else. Such "peace and co-operation" as Dr. Watts proposed would be peace and co-operation between him and Professor Tyndall, or between the theologians and the British Association, but "peace and co-operation between science and religion" is a term which carries absurdity on its face. Science is simply a body of facts which lead people familiar with them to infer the existence of certain laws. How can it, therefore, be either at peace or war with anybody, or co-operate with anybody? What Professor Tyndall might promise would be either not to discover any more facts, or to discover only certain classes of facts, or to draw no inferences from facts which would be unfavorable to Dr. Watts's theory of the universe; but the only result of this would be that Tyndall would lose his place as a scientific man, and others would go on discovering the facts and drawing the inferences.

In like manner, the supposition that Christianity can be defended against Positivism on grounds of expediency implies a singular conception of the mental operations of those persons who are affected by Positivist theories, and indeed, we might add, of the thinking world generally. No man believes in a religion simply because he thinks it useful, and therefore no man's real adhesion to the Christian creed can be secured by showing him how human happiness would suffer by its extinction.

This argument, if it had any weight at all, would only induce persons either to pretend to be Christians when they were not, or to refrain from assailing Christianity, or to avoid all inquiries which might possibly lead to sceptical conclusions. It is therefore, perhaps, a good argument to address to believers, because it may induce them to suppress doubts and avoid lines of thought or social relations likely to beget doubt; but it is an utterly futile argument to address to those who have already lost their faith. Men believe because they are convinced; it is not in their power to believe from motives of prudence or from public spirit.

However, the complaints of the theologians excited by Professor Tyndall's last utterances are not wholly unreasonable. Science has done nothing hitherto to give it any authority in the region of the unseen. "Beyond the boundary of experimental evidence" one man's vision is about as good as another's. It is interesting to know that Professor Tyndall there "discerns in matter the potency and promise of every quality and form of life," but only because he is a distinguished man, who gives much thought to this class of subjects and occupies a very prominent place in the public eye. As a basis for belief of any kind, his vision is of no more value than that of the Archbishop of Canterbury, who would probably in that region discern the promise and potency of every form of life in a supreme and creative intelligence. Scientific men are continually pushing back the limits of our knowledge of the material universe. They have during the last eighty years made an enormous addition to the sum of that knowledge, but they have not, since Democritus, taken away one hair's-breadth from the Mystery which lies behind. In fact, their labors have in many ways deepened this Mystery. We can appeal confidently to any candid man to say, for instance, whether Darwin's theory of the origin of life and the evolution of species does not make this globe and its inhabitants a problem vastly darker and more inscrutable than the Mosaic account of the creation. Take, again, the light thrown on the constitution of the sun by the spectroscope; it is a marvellous addition to our knowledge of our environment, but then, does it not make our ignorance as to the origin of the sun seem deeper? No scientific man pretends that any success in discovery will ever lead the human mind beyond the resolution of the number of laws which now seem to govern phenomena into a smaller number; but if we reached the limit of the possible in that direction to-morrow, we should be as far from the secret of the universe as ever. When we have all got to the blank wall which everybody admits lies at the boundary of experimental evidence, the philosopher will know no more about what lies beyond than the peasant, though the peasant will probably do then what he does now--people it with the creatures of his imagination. If a philosopher in our day likes to anticipate that period, and hazards the conjecture that matter lies beyond, he is welcome to his guess, but it ought to be understood that it is only a guess.

The danger to society from the men of science does not, we imagine, lie in the direction in which the theologians look for it. We do not think they need feel particularly troubled by Professor Tyndall's speculations as to the origin of things, for these speculations are very old, and have, after all, only a remote connection with human affairs. But there are signs both in his and Professor Huxley's methods of popularizing science, and in those of a good many of their followers, that we may fear the growth of something in the nature of a scientific priesthood, who, tempted by the great facilities for addressing the public which our age affords, and to which nearly every other profession has fallen a victim, will no longer confine themselves to their laboratories and museums and scientific journals, but serve as "ministers of nature" before great crowds of persons, for the most part of small knowledge and limited capacity, on whom their hints, suggestions, and denunciations will have a dangerously stimulating effect, particularly as the contempt of scientific men for what is called "literature"--that is, the recorded experience of the human race and the recorded expression of human feelings--grows every year stronger, and exerts more and more influence on the masses. The number of dabblers in science--of persons with a slight smattering of chemistry, geology, botany, and so on--too, promises to be largely increased for some time to come by the arrangements of one sort or another made by colleges and schools for scientific education; and though there is reason to expect from this education a considerable improvement in knowledge of the art of reasoning, there is also reason to fear a considerable increase of dogmatic temper, of eagerness for experimentation in all fields, and of scorn for the experience of persons who have never worked in the laboratory or done any deep-sea dredging. Now, whatever views we may hold as to the value of science in general and in the long run to the human race, and in particular its value for purposes of legislation and social economy, which we are far from denying, there is some risk that lectures like Professor Huxley's at Belfast, dressed up for promiscuous crowds, and produced with the polite scorn of infallibility, in which the destruction of moral responsibility is broadly hinted at as one of the probable results of researches in biology, will do great mischief. For what does it matter, or rather ought it to matter, for social purposes, in what part of a man's system his conscience lies, or whether pressure on a particular portion of the brain may convert him into a thief, when we know, as of experience, that the establishment of good courts and police turns a robbers' den into a hive of peaceful industry, and when we see the wonders which discipline works in an ignorant crowd?

THE CHURCH AND SCIENCE

A considerable body of the graduates of the Irish Catholic University, including members of the legal and medical professions, presented a long and solemn memorial to Cardinal Cullen and the other Catholic bishops at the late commencement of that institution, which throws a good deal of light not only on the vexed question of Catholic education in Ireland, but on the relations of the Catholic Church to education everywhere. The memorial examined in detail the management of the university, which it pronounces so bad as to endanger the existence of the college. But what it most complains of is the all but total absence of instruction in science. The memorialists say that the neglect of science by the university has afforded a very plausible argument to the enemies of the university, who never tire of repeating that the Catholic Church is the enemy of science, and that she will carry out her usual policy in Ireland with respect to it; that "no one can deny that the Irish Catholics are miserably deficient in scientific education, and that this deficiency is extremely galling to them; and, in a commercial sense, involves a loss to them, while, in an intellectual sense, it involves a positive degradation." They speak regretfully of the secession of Professor Sullivan, to take the presidency of the Queen's College, Cork, and declare that "no Irish-Catholic man of science can be found to take his place." They then go on to make several astounding charges. The lecture-list of the university does not include for the faculty of arts a single professor of the physical or natural sciences, or the name of a solitary teacher in descriptive geometry, geology, zoology, comparative anatomy, mineralogy, mining, astronomy, philology, ethnol-

ogy, mechanics, electricity, or optics. Of the prizes and exhibitions, the number offered in classics equals that of those offered in all other studies put together, while
in other universities the classical prizes do not exceed one-fourth of the whole.
They wind up their melancholy recital by declaring that they are determined that
the scientific inferiority of Irish Catholics shall not last any longer; and that if they
cannot obtain a scientific education in their own universities, they will seek it at
Trinity or the Queen's Colleges, or study it for themselves in the works of Haeckel,
Darwin, Huxley, Tyndall, and Lyell. They make one other singular complaint, viz.,
that no provision is made for supplying the lay students with instruction in theology.

It ought to be said in defence of the cardinal and the bishops, though the memorialists probably could not venture to say it, that the church hardly pretends
that the university is an efficient or complete instrument of education. It has been
in existence, it is true, twenty years, but the main object of its promoters during
this period has apparently been to harass or frighten the government by means of it
into granting them an endowment, or giving them control of the Queen's Colleges.
Had they succeeded in this, they would doubtless before now have made a show of
readiness to afford something in the nature of scientific instruction, because, as the
memorialists remark, there is no denying "that the physical and natural sciences
have become the chief studies of the age." But the memorialists must be either very
simple-minded or very ignorant Catholics, if they suppose that any endowment or
any pressure from public opinion would ever induce the Catholic hierarchy to undertake to turn out students who would make a respectable figure among the scientific graduates of other universities, or even hold their own among the common run
of amateur readers of Huxley and Darwin and Tyndall. There is no excuse for any
misunderstanding as regards the policy of the church on this point. She has never
given the slightest encouragement or sanction to the idea which so many Protestant
divines have of late years embraced, that theology is a progressive science, capable
of continued development in the light of newly discovered facts, and of gradual
adaptation to the changing phases of our knowledge of the physical universe. She
has hundreds of times given out as absolute truth a certain theory of the origin of
man and of the globe he lives on, and she cannot either abandon it or encourage
any study or habit of mind which would naturally or probably lead to doubt of the

correctness of this theory, or of the church's authority in enunciating it. In fact, the Pope, who is now an infallible judge in all matters of faith and discipline, has, within the last five years, in the famous "Syllabus" of modern follies, pronounced damnable and erroneous nearly all the methods and opinions by which Irish or any other Catholics could escape the deficiency in scientific knowledge which they say they find so injurious and so degrading. It is safe to say, therefore, that a Catholic cannot receive an education which would fit him to acquire distinction among scientific men in our day, without either incurring everlasting damnation or running the risk of it. Beside a danger of this kind, of course, as any priest will tell him, commercial loss and social inferiority are small matters.

Of course, if we take the facts of a great many branches of physical science by themselves, it would be easy enough to show that a good Catholic might safely accept them. But no man can reach these facts by investigations of his own, or hold to them intelligently and fruitfully, without acquiring intellectual habits and making use of tests which the church considers signs of a rebellious and therefore sinful temper. Moreover, nobody who has attained the limits of our present knowledge in chemistry, geology, comparative anatomy, ethnography, philology, and mythology can stand there with closed eyes. He must inevitably peer into the void beyond, and would be more than human if he did not indulge in speculations as to the history of the universe and its destiny which the church must treat as endangering his salvation. This is so well known that one reads the lamentations of these Catholic laymen with considerable surprise. They may be fairly supposed to know something of church history, and, even if they do not, they must profess some knowledge of the teaching given by the church in those universities of other countries which she controls. She does not encourage the study of natural science anywhere. Mathematics and astronomy she looks on with some favor, though we do not know how the spectroscope may have affected her toward the latter; and we venture to assert that these are the only fields of science in which any Catholic layman attains distinction without forfeiting his standing in the eyes of the clergy. We do not now speak of the French, Italian, and German Catholic laymen who go on with their investigations without caring whether the clergy like them or not, and without taking the trouble to make any formal repudiation of the church's authority over their intellects. We simply say there are no pious Catholic scientific men of any note, and never will be if the Catholic clergy can help it, and the lamentations of Catholics over the fact are logically absurd.

The legislation which Prussia is now putting into force on the subject of clerical education is founded on a candid recognition of the church's position on this matter. Prince Bismarck is well aware that in no seminary or college controlled by priests is there any chance that a young man will receive the best instruction of the day on the subjects in which the modern world is most interested, and by which the affairs of the State are most influenced. He has, therefore, wisely decided that it is the duty of the State to see that men who still exert as much power over popular thought as priests do, and are to receive State pay as popular instructors, shall also receive the best obtainable secular education before being subjected to purely professional training in the theological seminaries. The desperation of the fight made against him by the clergy is due to their well-grounded belief that in order to get a young man in our time to swallow a fair amount of Catholic theology, he must be caught early and kept close. The warfare which is raging in Prussia is one which has broken out in every country in which the government has formal relations with the church.

The appearance of a mutinous spirit among the Irish laity, and this not on political but scientific subjects, shows that the poison has sunk very deep and is very virulent; for the Irish laity have been until now the foremost Catholics in the world in silence and submissiveness, and there is nothing in ecclesiastical history which can equal in absurdity a request, addressed to Cardinal Cullen, that he would supply them with the kind of teaching which other men get from Tyndall and Huxley. With ecclesiastical insubordination arising out of differences on matters of doctrine or discipline, such as that manifested by the Old Catholics, it is comparatively easy to deal. Schismatics can be excommunicated by an authority which they have themselves venerated, and from an organization in which they loved to live and would fain have died. But over wanderers into the fields of science the church loses all hold. Her weapons are the jest of the museum and the laboratory, and her lore the babbling of the ignorant or blind.

THE CHURCH AND GOOD CONDUCT

The Episcopal Church, at the late Triennial Convention, took up and determined to make a more vigorous effort to deal with the problem presented by the irreligion of the poor and the dishonesty of church-members. It is an unfortunate and, at first sight, somewhat puzzling circumstance, that so many of the culprits in the late cases of fraud and defalcation should have been professing Christians, and in some cases persons of unusual ecclesiastical activity, and that this activity should apparently have furnished no check whatever to the moral descent. It is proposed to meet the difficulty by more preaching, more prayer, and greater use of lay assistance in church-work. There is nothing very new, however, about the difficulty. There is hardly a year in which it is not deplored at meetings of church organizations, and in which solemn promises are not made to devise some mode of keeping church-members up to their professions, and gathering more of the church-less working-classes into the fold; but somehow there is not much visible progress to be recorded. The church scandals multiply in spite of pastors and people, and the workingmen decline to show themselves at places of worship, although the number of places of worship and of church-members steadily increases.

We are sorry not to notice in any of the discussions on the subject a more frank and searching examination of the reason why religion does not act more powerfully as a rule of conduct. Until such an examination is made, and its certain results boldly faced by church reformers, the church cannot become any more of a help to right living than it is now, be this little or much. The first thing which such an examination would reveal is a thing which is in everybody's mind and on everybody's tongue in private, but which is apt to be evaded or only slightly alluded to at ecclesiastical synods and conventions--we mean the loss of faith in the dogmatic part of Christianity. People do not believe in the fall, the atonement, the resurrection, and a future state of reward and punishment at all, or do not believe in them with the certainty and vividness which are needed to make faith a constant influence on man's daily life. They do not believe they will be damned for sin with the assurance they once did, and they are consequently indifferent to most of what is said to them of the need of repentance. They do not believe the story of Christ's life and the theory of his character and attributes given in the New Testament, or they regard them as merely a picturesque background to his moral teachings, about which a Christian may avoid coming to any positive conclusion.

No man who keeps himself familiar with the intellectual and scientific movements of the day, however devout a Christian he may be, likes to question himself as to his beliefs about these matters, or would like to have to define accurately where his faith ended and his doubts began. If he is assailed in discussion by a sceptic and his combativeness roused, he will probably proclaim himself an implicit and literal acceptor of the gospel narratives; but he will not be able to maintain this mental attitude alone in his own room. The effort that has been made by Unitarians and others to meet this difficulty by making Christ's influence and authority rest on his moral teachings and example, without the support of a divine nature or mission or sacrifice, has failed. The Christian Church cannot be held together as a great social force by his teaching or example as a moral philosopher. A church organized on this theory speedily becomes a lecture association or a philanthropic club, of about as much aid to conduct as Freemasonry. Christ's sermons need the touch of supernatural authority to make them impressive enough for the work of social regeneration, and his life was too uneventful and the society in which he lived too simple, to give his example real power over the imagination of a modern man who regards him simply as a social reformer.

This decline of faith in Christian dogma and history has not, however, produced by any means a decline in religious sentiment, but it has deprived religion of a good deal of its power as a means of moral discipline. Moral discipline is acquired mainly by the practice of doing what one does not like to do, under the influence of mastering fear or hope. The conquest of one's self, of which Christian moralists speak so much, is simply the acquisition of the power of doing easily things to which one's natural inclinations are opposed; and in this work the mass of mankind are powerfully aided--indeed, we may say, have to be aided--by the prospect of reward or punishment. The wonderful results which are achieved in the army, by military authority, in inspiring coarse and common natures with a spirit of the loftiest devotion, are simply due to the steady application by day and by night of a punishing and rewarding authority. The loss of this, or its great enfeeblement, undoubtedly has deprived the church of a large portion of its means of discipline, and reduced it more nearly to the *role* of a stimulater and gratifier of certain tender emotions. It contains a large body of persons whose religious life consists simply of a succession of sensations not far removed from one's enjoyment of music and poetry; and another large body, to whom it furnishes refuge and consolation of a vague and ill-defined sort in times of sorrow and disappointment. To these persons the church prayers and hymns are not trumpet-calls to the battle-field, but soothing melodies, which give additional zest to home comforts and luxuries, and make the sharper demands of a life of the highest integrity less unbearable. Nay, the case is rather worse than this. We have little doubt that this sentimental religion, as we may call it, in many cases deceives a man as to his own moral condition, and hides from him the true character and direction of the road he is travelling, and furnishes his con-science with a false bottom. The revelations of the last few years as to its value as a guide in the conduct of life have certainly been plain and deplorable.

The evil in some degree suggests the remedy, though we do not mean to say that we know of any complete remedy. Church-membership ought to involve dis-cipline of some kind in order to furnish moral aid. It ought, that is to say, to impose some restraint on people's inclinations, the operation of which will be visible, and enforced by some external sanction. If, in short, Christians are to be regarded as more trustworthy and as living on a higher moral plane than the rest of the world, they must furnish stronger evidence of their sincerity than is now exacted from them, in the shape of plain and open self-denial. The church, in short, must be an organization held together by some stronger ties than enjoyment of weekly music and oratory in a pretty building, and alms-giving which entails no sacrifice and is often only a tickler of social vanity. There is in monasticism a suggestion of the way in which it must retain its power over men's lives, and be enabled to furnish them with a certificate of character. Its members will have to have a good deal of the as-cetic about them, but without any withdrawal from the world.

How to attain this without sacrificing the claims of art, and denying the legiti-macy of honestly acquired material power, and, in fact, restricting individual free-dom to a degree which the habits and social theories of the day would make very odious, is the problem to be solved, and, it is, no doubt, a very tough one. General inculcation of "plain living" will not solve it, as long as "plain living" is not defined and the "self-made man" who has made a great fortune and spends it lavishly is held up to the admiration of every school-boy. The church has been making of late years a gallant effort to provide accommodation for the successful, and enable them to be good Christians without sacrificing any of the good things of this life, and, in fact, without surrendering anything they enjoy, or favoring the outside public with any recognizable proof of their sincerity. We do not say that this is reprehensible, but it is easy to see that it has the seeds of a great crop of scandals in it. Donations in an age of great munificence, and horror of far-off or unattractive sins, like the slaveholding of Southerners and the intemperance of the miserable poor, are not, and ought not to be, accepted as signs of inward and spiritual grace, and of readiness to scale "the toppling crags of duty."

The conversion of the working-classes, too, it is safe to say, will never be accomplished by any ecclesiastical organization which sells cushioned pews at auction, or rents them at high rates, and builds million-dollar churches for the accommodation of one thousand worshippers. The passion for equality has taken too strong hold of the workingman to make it possible to catch him with cheap chapels and assistant pastors. He will not seek salvation *in forma pauperis*, and thinks the best talent in the ministerial market not a whit too good for him. He not unnaturally doubts the sincerity of Christians who are not willing to kneel beside badly dressed persons in prayer on the one day of the week when prayer is public. In fact, to fit the Protestant Church in this country to lay hold of the laboring population a great process of reconstruction would be necessary. The congregational system would have to be abandoned or greatly modified, the common fund made larger and administered in a different way. There would have, in short, to be a close approach to the Roman Catholic organization, and the churches would have to lose the character of social clubs, which now makes them so comfortable and attractive. Well-to-do Christians would have to sacrifice their tastes in a dozen ways, and give up the expectation of aesthetic pleasure in public worship. There cannot be a vast Gothic cathedral for the multitude in every city. The practice of the church would have to be forced up to its own theory of its character and mission, which would involve serious collision with some of the most deeply rooted habits and ideas of modern social and political life. That there is any immediate probability of this we do not believe. Until it is brought about, its members must make up their minds to have religious professions treated by some as but slight guarantees of character, and by others as but cloaks of wrong-doing, hard as this may be for that large majority to whom they are an honest expression of sure hopes and noble aims.

ROLE OF THE UNIVERSITIES IN POLITICS

Mr. Galton, in his work on "Hereditary Genius," has drawn attention in a striking chapter to the effect which the systematic destruction and expatriation, by the Inquisition or the religious intolerance of the government, of the leading men of the nation--its boldest thinkers, most ardent investigators, most prudent and careful and ingenious workers, in generation after generation--had in bringing about the moral and political decline of the three great Latin countries, France, Spain, and Italy--a decline of which, in the case of the two former at least, we have probably not seen the end. The persons killed or banished amounted only to a few thousands every year, but they were--no matter from what rank they came--the flower of the population: the men whose labor and whose influence enabled the State to keep its place in the march of civilization. The picture is very valuable (particularly just now, when there is so great a disposition to revel in the consciousness of vast numbers), as calling attention to the smallness of the area within which, after all, the sources of national greatness and progress are to be sought. The mind which keeps the mass in motion, which saves and glorifies it, would most probably, if we could lay bare the secret of national life, be found in the possession of a very small proportion of the people, though not in any class in particular-- neither among the rich nor the poor, the learned nor simple, capitalists nor laborers; but the abstraction of these few from the sum of national existence, though it would hardly be noticed in the census, would produce a fatal languor, were the nation not constantly receiving fresh blood from other countries.

This element was singled out with considerable accuracy in France and Spain by religious persecution. It would happily be impossible to devise any process of selection one-quarter as efficient in our age or in this country. The one we have been using for the last twenty years, and on which a good deal of popular reliance has been placed, is the accumulation of wealth; and under this "the self-made man"-

-that is, the man who, starting in life ignorant and poor, has made a large fortune, and got control of a great many railroads and mines and factories--has risen into the front rank of eminence. The events of the last five years, however, have had a damaging effect on his reputation, and he now stands as low as his worst enemies could desire. As he declines, the man of some kind of training naturally rises; and it would be running no great risk to affirm that the popular mind inclines more than it has usually done to the belief that trained men--that is, men who have been prepared for their work by teaching on approved methods--are after all the most valuable possession a country can have, and that a country is well or ill off in proportion as they are numerous or the reverse. One does not need to travel very far from this position to reach the conclusion that there is probably no way in which we could strike so deadly a blow at the happiness and progress of the United States as by sweeping away, by some process of proscription kept up during a few generations, the graduates of the principal colleges. In no other way could we make so great a drain on the reserved force of character, ambition, and mental culture which constitutes so large a portion of the national vitality. They would not be missed at the polls, it is true, and if they were to run a candidate for the Presidency to-morrow their vote would excite great merriment among the politicians; but if they were got rid of regularly for forty or fifty years in the manner we have suggested, and nothing came in from the outside to supply their places, the politicians would somehow find that they themselves had less public money to vote or steal, less national aspiration to trade upon, less national force to direct, less national dignity to maintain or lose, and that, in fact, by some mysterious process, they were getting to be of no more account in the world than their fellows in Guatemala or Costa Rica.

There will come to the colleges of the United States during the next fifty years a larger and larger number of men who either strongly desire training for themselves or are the sons of men who are deeply sensible of its advantages, and therefore are at the head of families which possess and appreciate the traditions of high civilization, and would like to live in them and contribute their share to perpetuating them-- and they will not come from any one portion of the country. There are, unhappily, "universities" in all parts of the Union, but there is hardly a doubt that as the means of communication are improved and cheapened, and as the real nature and value of the university education become better understood, the tendency to use the small local institutions passing by this name as, what they really are, high schools, and resort to the half-dozen colleges which can honestly call themselves universities, will increase. The demands which modern culture, owing to the advance of science and research in every field, now makes on a university, in the shape of professors, books, apparatus, are so great that only the largest and wealthiest institutions can pretend to meet them, and in fact there is something very like false pretence in the promise to do so held out to poor students by many of the smaller colleges. These colleges doubtless do a certain amount of work very creditably; but they are uncandid in saying that they give a university education, and in issuing diplomas purporting to be certificates that any such education has either been sought or received. The idea of maintaining a university for the sake of the local glory of it is a form of folly which ought not to be associated with education in any stage. These considerations are now felt to be so powerful in other countries that they threaten the destruction of a whole batch of universities in Italy which have come down famous and honored from the Middle Ages and have sent out twenty generations of students, and they are causing even the very best of the smaller universities in Germany, great and efficient as many of them are, to tremble for their existence.

There is no interest of learning, therefore, which would not be served by the greater concentration of the resources of the country as regards university education, still less is there any interest of society or politics. It is of the last importance that the class of men from all parts of the country whom the universities send out into the world should as far as possible be educated together, and start on their careers with a common stock of traditions, tastes, and associations. Much as steam and the telegraph have done, and will do, to diminish for administrative purposes the size of the Republic, and to simplify the work of government, they cannot prevent the creation of a certain diversity of interests, and even of temperament and manners, through differences of climate and soil and productions. There will never come a time when we shall not have more or less of such folly as the notion that the South and West need more money than the East, because they have less capital, or the struggle of some parts of the country for a close market against other parts which seek an open one. Nothing but a reign of knowledge and wisdom, such as centuries will not bring, will prevent States on the Gulf or on the Pacific from fancying that their interests are not identical with those of the Northern Atlantic, and nothing but profound modifications in the human constitution will ever bring the California wheat-raiser into complete sympathy with the New England shoemaker.

The work of our political system for ages to come will consist largely in keeping these differences in check; and in doing it, it will need all the help it can get from social and educational influences. It ought to be the aim, therefore, of the larger institutions of learning to offer every inducement in their power to students from all parts of the Union, and more especially from the South, as the region which is most seriously threatened by barbarism, and in which the sense of national unity and the hold of national traditions on the popular mind are now feeblest. We at the North owe to the civilized men at the South who are now, no matter what their past faults or delusions may have been, struggling to save a large portion of the Union from descent into heathen darkness and disorder, the utmost help and consideration. We owe them above all a free and generous welcome to a share in whatever means of culture we have at our disposal, and ought to offer it, as far as is consistent with our self-respect, in a shape that will not wound theirs.

The question of the manner of doing this came up incidentally at Harvard the other day, at the dedication of the great hall erected in memory of the graduates of the university who died in the war. The hall is to be used for general college purposes, for examinations, and some of the ceremonial of commencement, as well as for dinner, and a portion of the walls is covered with tablets bearing the names of those to whose memory it is dedicated. The question whether the building would keep alive the remembrance of the civil war in any way in which it is inexpedient to keep it alive, or in any way which would tend to keep Southern students away from the university, has been often asked, and by some answered in the affirmative. General Devens, who presided at the alumni dinner, gave full and sufficient answer to those who find fault with the rendering of honor on the Northern side to those who fell in its cause; but General Bartlett--who perhaps more than any man living is qualified to speak for those who died in the war--uttered, in a burst of unpremeditated eloquence, at the close of the proceedings, the real reason why no Southern man need, and we hope will never, feel hurt by Northern memorials of the valor and constancy of Northern soldiers. It is not altogether the cause which ennobles fighting; it is the spirit in which men fight; and no horror of the objects of the Southern insurrection need prevent anybody from admiring or lamenting the gallant men who honestly, loyally, and from a sense of duty perished in its service. It is not given to the wisest and best man to choose the right side; but the simplest and humblest knows whether it is his conscience which bids him lay down his life. And this test may be applied by each side to all the victims of the late conflict without diminishing by one particle its faith in the justice of its own cause. Moreover, as General Bartlett suggested, the view of the nature of the struggle which is sure to gain ground all over the country as the years roll on is that it was a fierce and passionate but inevitable attempt to settle at any cost a controversy which could be settled in no other way; and that all who shared in it, victors or vanquished, helped to save the country and establish its government on sure and lasting foundations. This feeling cannot grow without bringing forcibly to mind the fact that the country was saved through the war that virtue might increase, that freedom might spread and endure, and that knowledge might rule, and not that politicians might have a treasury to plunder and marble halls to exchange their vituperation in; thus uniting the best elements of Northern and Southern society by the bonds of honest indignation as well as of noble hopes.

THE HOPKINS UNIVERSITY

The ***Baltimore American***, discussing the plan of the Hopkins University in that city, says: "The ***Nation*** suggests to the Board of Trustees a university that would leave Latin, Greek, mathematics, and the elements of natural science out of its curriculum." This is so great a mistake that we are at a loss to understand how it could have been made. The ***Nation*** has never suggested anything of the kind. The university which the ***Nation*** has expressed the hope the trustees would found is simply a university with such a high standard for admission on all subjects that the professors would be saved the necessity of teaching the rudiments of either Latin, Greek, mathematics, or natural science; or, in other words, that the country would be saved considerable waste of skilled labor. The reason why we have ventured to expect this of the Hopkins trustees is that they enjoy the all but unprecedented advantage of being left in possession of a very large bequest, with complete liberty, within very wide limits, as to the disposition of it. In other words, they are to found a university with it, but as to the kind of university they may exercise their discretion.

That this is a very exceptional position everybody familiar with the history of American colleges knows. All the older colleges are bound to the state, or to certain religious denominations, by laws or usages or precedents which impose a certain tolerably fixed character either on the subjects or on the mode of teaching them, or on both. They have traditions to uphold, or denominational interests to care for, or political prejudices to satisfy. The newer ones, on the other hand, are apt to have incurred a bondage even worse still, in having to carry out the wishes of a founder who, in ninety-nine cases out of a hundred, had only a faint notion of the nature and needs of a university, and in endowing one sought rather to erect a monument to his memory than to found a seat of learning. In so far as he was interested in the curriculum, he probably desired that it should be such as would satisfy some want which he himself felt, or thought he felt, in early life, or should diffuse some social or religious or political crotchet on which his fancy had secretly fed during his years of active exertion, and on the success of which he came to think, in the latter part of his life, that the best interests of the community were dependent. The number of these honorably ambitious but ill-informed and somewhat eccentric testators increases every year, as the country grows in wealth and the habit of giving to public objects gains in strength.

The consequence is that we are threatened with the spectacle during the coming century of a great waste of money by well-meaning persons in the establishment all over the country of institutions calling themselves "universities," which are either so feebly equipped as rather to hinder than help the cause of education, or so completely committed by their organization to the propagation of certain social or religious theories as to deserve the appellation of mission stations rather than of colleges. Education is now an art of exceeding delicacy and complexity. To master it, so as to have a trustworthy opinion as to the relative value of studies and as to the best mode of pursuing them, and as to the organization of institutions devoted to the work of instruction, a man needs both learning and experience. The giving him money to employ in his special work, therefore, without leaving him discretion as to the manner in which he shall use it, is to prepare almost certainly for its waste in more than one direction. To make the most of the resources of the country for educational purposes, it is necessary above all things that they should be placed at the disposal of those who have made education a special study, and who are free, as we understand the Hopkins trustees to be, from any special bias or bond, and are ready or willing to look at the subject from every side. Their liberty, of course, brings with it great responsibility--all the greater for the reasons we have been enumerating.

Now, as to the use which they should make of this liberty, the ***Baltimore American*** fears that if they found a university of the class sketched by us some weeks ago, "the people of Maryland would be greatly disappointed--there would not be over fifty students," and "there would be a great outcry against the investment of three and a half millions of dollars for the benefit of so small a number." Whether the people of Maryland will be disappointed or not, depends on the amount of consideration they give the matter. If they are satisfied that the foundation of such a university as is now talked of is the best use that can be made of the money, they will not be disappointed, and there will be no "outcry" at all. Being an intelligent people, they will on reflection see that the value of a university by no means depends solely on the proportion borne by the number of its students to the amount of its revenues, because, judged in this way--that is, as instruments of direct popular benefit--all the universities in the country might be pronounced failures. The bulk of the community derives no direct benefit from them at all. Harvard, for instance, has an endowment of about five million dollars, we believe, and the total number of the students is only 1,200, while the population of the State of Massachusetts is 1,500,000, so that, even supposing all the students to come from Massachusetts, which they do not, less than one person in every thousand profits by the university.

The same story might be told of Yale or any other college. Considered as what are called popular institutions--that is, institutions from which everybody can or does derive some calculable, palpable benefit--the universities of this and every other country are useless, and there ought on this theory to be a prodigious "outcry" against them, and they ought, on the principle of equality, if allowed to exist at all, to be allowed to exist only on condition that they will give a degree, or at least offer an education, to every male citizen of sound mind. But nobody takes this view of them. The poorest and most ignorant hod-carrier would not hold, if asked, that because he cannot go to college there ought to be no colleges. Sensible people in every country acknowledge that a high education can in the nature of things be only obtained by a very small proportion of the population; but that the few who seek it, and can afford to take it, should get it, and should get it of the best quality, they hold to be a public benefit. Now, why a public benefit? The service that Harvard or Yale renders to the community certainly does not lie simply in the fact that it qualifies a thousand young men every year to earn a livelihood. They would earn a livelihood whether they went to college or not. The vast majority of men earn a livelihood without going to college or thinking of it. Indeed, it is doubted by many persons, and with much show of reason, whether a man does not earn it all the more readily for not going to college at all; and as regards the work of the world of all kinds, the great bulk of it is done, and well done, by persons who have not received a university education and do not regret it. So that the benefits which the country derives from the universities consists mainly in the refining and elevating influences which they create, in the taste for study and research which they diffuse, in the social and political ideals which they frame and hold up for admiration, in the confidence in the power of knowledge which they indirectly spread among the people, and in the small though steady contributions they make to that reverence for "things not seen" in which the soul of the state may be said to lie, and without which it is nothing better than a factory or an insurance company.

There is nothing novel about the considerations we are here urging. The problem over which university reformers have been laboring in every country during the past forty years has been, how to rid the universities, properly so called, of the care of the feeble, inefficient, and poorly prepared students, and reserve their teaching for the better-fitted, older, and more matured; or, in other words, how, in the interest both of economy and culture, to reserve the highest teaching power of the community for the most promising material. It is forty years since John Stuart Mill wrote a celebrated attack on the English universities, then in a very low condition, in which he laid it down broadly that the end above all for which endowed universities ought to exist was "to keep alive philosophy," leaving "the education of common minds for the common business of life" for the most part to private enterprise. This seemed at the time exacting too much, and it doubtless seems so still; but it is nevertheless true that ever since that period universities of the highest class, both in Europe and in this country, have been working in that direction--striving, that is to say, either to sift the applicants for admission, by imposing increasingly severe tests, and thus presenting to the professors only pupils of the highest grade to work upon; or, at all events, if not repelling the ill-fitted, expending all their strength in furnishing the highest educational advantages to the well-fitted. In the last century, Harvard and Yale were doing just the kind of work that the high schools now do--that is, taking young lads and teaching them the elements of literature. At the present day they are throwing this work as far as possible on the primary schools, and reserving their professors and libraries and apparatus, as far as the state of the country and the conditions of their organization will permit, for those older and more advanced students who bring to the work of learning both real ardor and real preparation. A boy has to know more to get into either of them to-day than his grandfather knew when he graduated. Nevertheless, with all the efforts they can make after this true economy of power and resources, there is in both of them a large amount of waste of labor. There are men in both of them, and in various other colleges, much of whose work is almost as much a misuse of energy and time as if they were employed so many hours a day in carrying hods of mortar, simply because they are doing what the masters of primary schools ought to do, and what no man at a university ought to be asked to do. It is a kind of work, too, which, if it have to be done in colleges at all, is already abundantly provided for by endowment. No Maryland youth who desires to learn a little mathematics, get a smattering of classics, and some faint notions of natural science, or even to support himself by manual labor while doing this, will suffer if the Hopkins endowment is used for higher work. The country swarms already with institutions which meet his needs, and in which he can graduate with ease to himself and credit to his State. The trustees of this one will do him and the State and the whole country most service, therefore, by providing a place to which, after he has got hold of the rudiments at some other college, he can come, if he has the right stuff in him, and pursue to the end the studies for which all universities should really be reserved.

THE SOUTH AFTER THE WAR
I

September 8, 1877.

Having just returned from a few weeks' stay in Virginia it has occurred to me as probable that your readers would be interested in hearing how such changes in Southern manners and tone of thought and economical outlook as could be noted in a brief visit strike one who had travelled in that region before the war had revolutionized it. It is now twenty years since I spent a winter traversing the Cotton States on horseback, sleeping at the house which happened to be nearest when the night caught me. Buchanan had just been elected; the friends of slavery, though anxious, were exultant and defiant, and the possibility of a separate political future had begun to take definite shape in the public mind, at least in the Gulf States. I am unable to compare the economical condition of that part of the country at that time with its condition to-day, because both slavery and agriculture in Virginia differed then in many important respects from slavery and agriculture farther south. But the habits and modes of thought and feeling bred by slavery were essentially the same all over the South; and I do not think that I shall go far astray in assuming that the changes in these which I have noticed in Virginia would be found to-day in all the other States.

The first which struck me, and it was a most agreeable one, was what I may call the emancipation which conversation and social intercourse with Northerners had undergone. In 1857 the tone of nearly everybody with whom I came in contact, however veiled by politeness, was in some degree irritable and defiant. My host and I were never long before the evening fire without my finding that he was impatient to talk about slavery, that he suspected me of disliking it, and yet that he wished to have me understand that he did not care, and that nobody at the South cared two cents what I thought about it, and that it was a little impertinent in me, who knew so little of the negro, to have any opinion about it at all. I was obliged, too, to confess inwardly that there was a good deal of justification for his bad temper. There was I, a curious stranger, roving through his country and eating at his board, and all the while secretly or openly criticising or condemning his relations with his laborers and servants, and, in fact, the whole scheme of his domestic life. I was not a pleasant companion, and nothing could make me one, and no matter on what themes our talk ran, it was colored by our opinions on the institution. He looked at nearly everything in politics and society from what might be called the slaveholder's point of view, and suspected me, on the other hand, of disguising reprobation of the South and its institutions in any praise of the North or of France or England which I might utter. So that there was a certain acridity and a sense of strong and deep limitations and reserves in our discussions, somewhat like those which are felt in the talk of a pious evangelical Protestant with a pious Catholic.

In Virginia of to-day I was conscious of a curious change in the atmosphere, as if the windows of a close room had been suddenly opened. I found that I was in a country where all things were debatable, and where I had not to be on the look-out for susceptibilities. The negro, too, about whom I used to have to be so careful, with whom I used to make it a point of honor not to talk privately or apart from his master when I was staying on a plantation, was wandering about loose, as it were, and nobody seemed to care anything about him any more than about any poor man. I found every Southerner I spoke to as ready to discuss him as to discuss sheep or oxen, to let you have your own views about him just as you had them about sheep or oxen. Moreover, I found instead of the stereotyped orthodox view of his place and capacity which prevailed in 1857, a great variety of opinions about him, mostly depreciatory, it is true, but still varying in degree as well as in kind. It is difficult to give anyone who has never had any experience of the old slave society an idea of the difference this makes in a stranger's position at the South. In short, as one Southerner expressed it to me on my mentioning the change, "Yes, sir, we have been brought into intellectual and moral relations with the rest of the civilized world." All subjects are now open at the South in conversation.

Is this true? it will probably be asked, with regard to the late war. Can you talk freely about that? Not exactly; but then the limitations on your discourse on this point are not peculiar to the South; they are such as would be put upon the discourse of two parties to a bloody contest in any civilized country among well-bred men or women. The events of the war you can discuss freely, but you are hardly at liberty to denounce Southern soldiers or officers, or accuse them of "rebellion," or to assume that they fought for base or wicked motives. Moreover, in a certain sense, all Southerners are still "unrepentant rebels." Doubtless, in view of the result, they will acknowledge that the war was a gigantic mistake; but I found that if I sought for an admission that, if it was all to do over again, they would not fight, I was touching on a very tender point, and I was gently but firmly repelled. The reason is plain enough. In confessing this, they would, they think, be confessing that their sons and brothers and fathers had perished miserably in a causeless struggle on which they ought never to have entered, and this, of course, would look like a slur on their memory, and their memory is still, after the lapse of twelve years, very sacred and very dear. I doubt if many people at the North have an adequate notion of the intensity of the emotions with which Southerners look back on the war; and I mean tender and not revengeful or malignant emotions. The losses of the battle-field were deeply felt at the North--in many households down to the very roots of life; but on the whole they fell on a large and prosperous population, on a community which in the very thick of the fray seemed to be rolling up wealth, which revelled as it fought, and came out of the battle triumphant, exultant, and powerful. At the South they swept through a scanty population with the most searching destructiveness, and when all was over they had to be wept over in ruined homes and in the midst of a society which was wrecked from top to bottom, and in which all relatives and friends had sunk together to common perdition. There has been no other such cataclysm in history. Great states have been conquered before now, but conquest did not mean a sudden and desolating social revolution; so that to a Southerner the loss of relatives on the battle-field or in the hospital is associated with the loss of everything else. A gentleman told me of his going, at the close of the war, into a little church in South Carolina on Sunday, and finding it filled with women, who were all in black, and who cried during the singing. It reminded one of the scene in the cathedral at Leyden, when the people got together to chant a *Te Deum* on hearing that the besieging army was gone; but, the music suddenly dying out, the air was filled with the sounds of sobbing. The Leydeners, however, were weak and half-starved people, weeping over a great deliverance; these South Carolinians were weeping before endless bereavement and hopeless poverty. I doubt much if any community in the modern world was ever so ruthlessly brought face to face with what is sternest and hardest in human life; and those of them who have looked at it without flinching have something which any of us may envy them.

But then I think it would be a mistake to suppose that Southerners came out of the war simply sorrowful. At the close, and for some time afterward, they undoubtedly felt fiercely and bitterly, and hated while they wept; and this was the primal difficulty of reconstruction. Frequently in conversation I heard some violent speech or act occurring soon after the war mentioned with the parenthetical explanation, "You know, I felt very bitterly at that time." But, then, I have always heard it from persons who are to day good-tempered, conciliatory, and hopeful, and desirous of cultivating good relations with Northerners; from which the inference, which so many Northern politicians find it so hard to swallow, is easy--viz., that time produces on Southerners its usual effects. What Mr. Boutwell and Mr. Blaine would have us believe is that Southerners are a peculiar breed of men, on whom time produces no effect whatever, and who feel about things that happened twenty years ago just as they feel about things which happened a month ago.

The fact is, however, that they are in this respect like the rest of the human race. Time has done for their hearts and heads what it has done for the old Virginia battle-fields. There was not in 1865 a fence standing between the Potomac and Gordonsville, and but few, if any, undamaged houses. When I passed Manassas Junction the other day there was a hospitable-looking tavern and several houses at the station; the flowers were blooming in the yard, and crowds of young men and women in their Sunday clothes were gathered from the country around to see a base-ball match, and a well-tilled and well-fenced and smiling farming country stretched before my eyes in every direction. The only trace of the old fights was a rude graveyard filled, as a large sign informed us, with "the Confederate dead." All the rest of the way down to the springs the road ran through farms which looked as prosperous and peaceful as if the tide of war had not rolled over them inside a hundred years, and it is impossible to talk with the farmers ten minutes without seeing how thoroughly human and Anglo-Saxon they are. With them the war is history--tender, touching, and heroic history if you will, but having no sort of connection with the practical life of to-day. Some of us at the North think their minds are occupied with schemes for the assassination and spoliation of negroes, and for a "new rebellion." Their minds are really occupied with making money, and the farms show it, and their designs on the negro are confined to getting him to work for low wages. His wages are low--forty cents a day and rations, which cost ten cents--but he is content with it. I saw negroes seeking employment at this rate, and glad to get it; and in the making of the bargain nothing could be more commercial, apparently, than the relations of the parties. They were evidently laborer and employer to each other, and nothing more.

The state of things on two farms which I visited may serve as illustrations of the process of regeneration which is going on all over Virginia. They are two hundred miles apart. On one of two thousand acres there were, before the war, about one hundred and fifty slaves of all ages. The owner, at emancipation, put them in wagons and deposited them in Ohio. His successor now works the plantation with twelve hired men, who see to his cattle, of which he raises and feeds large herds. His cultivation is carried on on shares by white tenants. He has an overseer, makes a snug income, and spends a good part of his winters in Baltimore and New York. He laughs when you ask him if he regrets slavery. Nothing would induce him to take care of one hundred and fifty men, women, and children, furnishing perhaps thirty able-bodied men, littering the house with a swarm of lazy servants, and making heavy drafts on the meat-house and corn-crib, and running up doctor's bills.

The other was owned at the close of the war by a regular "Virginia gentleman," with the usual swarm of negroes, and who was in debt. He sold it to an enterprising young farmer from another county, paid his debts, and retired to a small place, where, with two or three hired men, he makes a living. The young farmer, instead of seventy-five slaves, works it with twelve hands in the busy season and three in winter, is up at five o'clock in the morning superintending them himself, raises all raisable crops, and is as intent on the markets and the experiments made by his neighbors as if he lived in Illinois or the Carse of Gowrie. He was led by Colonel Waring's book to try tile-draining, and made the tiles for the purpose on his own land. He was so successful that he now manufactures and soils tiles extensively to others. It would be difficult to meet at the North or in England two men with their faces turned away from the old times more completely than these, more averse from the old plantation ways; and, as far as I could learn or hear, they are fair specimens of the kind of men who are taking possession of the Old Dominion. Their neighbors consist of three classes: men who had by extraordinary exertions saved some or all of their land after the war, and had by borrowing or economizing managed to stock it, and are now prospering, by dint of close management and constant attention, on the Northern plan; young and enterprising men who had bought at low rates from original proprietors whom the war left hopelessly involved, and too old or incapable to recover; and a sprinkling of Northern and English immigrants.

II

The part played by the Virginia springs in the political and social life of "the States lately in rebellion," is to a traveller most interesting. The attraction of these springs to Southerners has been in times past, and is still, largely due to the fact that the South has, properly speaking, no other watering-places. Seaside resorts there are none worth mention, from Norfolk down to Mexico, and there are but few points of the long, level, dull, and sandy coast-line which are not more or less unhealthy. Suspicion on this point even hangs around the places in Florida now frequented by Northerners for the sake of the mild winter temperature. But oven if the sea-coast were healthy, it is in summer too hot to be attractive, and offers no relief to persons whose livers and kidneys have got out of order in the lowlands. These naturally seek the hills for coolness, and they go to the sulphur springs of Virginia because the sulphur waters are very powerful and efficacious in their effects on people afflicted with what the doctors call "hepatic troubles." But then they never would or could have gone from the Southern seaboard to places so far off if it had not been for the inestimable negro. The extent to which he contributed to the rapid pushing out of the scanty white population of the slave States to the Mississippi has never, I think, received due attention. He robbed pioneering, indeed, at the South of most of the hardship with which it is associated in the Northern mind--I was going to say discomfort as well as hardship, but this would be going too far. To the Southern planter, however, who could go West with a party of stalwart negroes to do the clearing, building, ploughing, and cooking and washing, the wilderness had but few of the terrors it presented to the Northern frontiersman. He was speedily provided with a very tolerable home; not certainly the kind of home which the taste of a man as well off at the North would be satisfied with, but a vastly better one than any new settler in the Northwestern States ever had. The springs in the Virginia mountains became popular a century ago, and were greatly resorted to in much the same way. They were remote and in the woods, but, owing to slavery, they swarmed from the very first with servants who could not "give notice" if they did not like the place, or felt lonesome.

The first accommodation at the springs consisted of a circle of log-cabins with a dining-hall and ball-room in the centre, and this constitutes the fundamental plan of a spring to this day. There is now always a hotel in which a considerable number of the visitors both sleep and eat, but the bulk of them, or a very large proportion of them, still live in the long rows of one-storied wooden huts, with galleries running along in front of the doors, which are dignified with the name of "cottages," but are in reality simply the log-cabin in the next stage of evolution; and the hotel has taken the place of the original dining and ball-rooms to which all resorted. In looking at the cottages, and thinking of the log-cabins which preceded them, and seeing what rude places they are, one wonders a little how people could ever have been, or can now be, induced to leave comfortable homes for the purpose of spending long summers in them. But this brings up one of the marked characteristics of Southern life, namely, the extent to which nearly all Southern men and women were led in the slavery days to associate comfort not with the trimness and order of Northern or English homes, but with an abundance of service. Well-to-do Northerners used to be surprised, in fact, at the amount of what they would consider discomfort in the way of rude or unfinished surroundings, hard beds, poor fare, want of order of all sorts, which even Southerners in easy circumstances were willing to put up with; but the explanation lay in the fact that Southerners placed their luxury in having plenty of servants at command. All the ladies had maids and the men "body servants" wherever they went, and this saved them, even on the frontier, from a great deal of drudgery and inconvenience. Even a log-cabin is not a bad place to lodge in if you have a valet (who cannot leave you) to dress you, and brush your boots and your clothes, and light your fire, and bring you ice-water and juleps and cocktails, and anything else you happen to think of, who sleeps comfortably in a blanket across your door. In fact, without this the Virginia springs could never have become a popular resort until railroads were opened. People used to take twenty days in reaching them from the coast-- some in their own carriages with four horses, and a wagon for the baggage and "darkies," and some in stages, sleeping in taverns on the roadside; but nothing could have made this practicable or tolerable but the band of negroes by whom they were always accompanied. This, too, enabled them to make their plans with certainty for staying at the springs all summer, which they could not have done had they been unable to count on their servants. One gentleman, a Charlestonian, telling me his reminiscences of these long journeys to the springs taken with his parents in their own carriage, when he was a boy, said his mother was very delicate and her health required it. This at the North would have been a joke, as it would have killed a delicate woman to go into the woods with hired "help" or without any service at all.

Partly owing to the efficacy of the waters and partly to the absence of other Southern watering-places, the springs became very early the resort of every Southerner who could afford to leave home in the summer, and they grew in favor owing to the peculiarities of Southern society and the delicate state of Southern relations with the North. In the first place, at the South people know each other, and know about each other, in a way of which the inhabitants of a denser and busier community have little idea. The number of persons in Illinois, or Ohio, or Michigan that a New Yorker knows anything about, or cares to see for social purposes, is exceedingly small. At the South everybody with the means to travel has relatives or friends or acquaintances of longer or shorter standing, in nearly every Southern State, whom it is agreeable for him to meet, and he knows that they will probably, at some part of the season or other, appear at the springs. They will not go North because the North is far away, is, in a certain sense, a strange community, and before the war a hostile or critical one. Then, too, the South abounded or abounds with local notables to a degree of which we have no idea at the North, with persons of a certain weight and consequence in their own State or county, and to whom this weight and consequence are so agreeable and important that they cannot bear to part with them when they go on a journey. They could always carry them with them to the springs. There everybody was sure to know their standing, while if they had gone up North they would be lost in the crowd and be nobodies, and, before the war, have been deprived of the services of their "body servants" or labored under constant anxiety about their security.

The springs, too, became, very early, and are now, a great marrying-place. The "desirable young men, all riding on horses," as the prophet called the Assyrian swells, go there in search of wives, and are pretty sure to find there all the marriageable young women of the South who can be said in any sense to be in society. Widows abound at the springs just now--by which I mean widows who would not object to trying the chances of matrimony again. I have been told that, since the war, it is not uncommon for families whose means are small to make up a purse to send one attractive youth or maid or forlorn widow to the springs, in the hope that during the season they may find the unknown soul which is to complete their destiny, somewhat like the "culture" donations made to promising people at the North to enable them to visit Europe. Then, too, to that very large proportion of the population at the South who lead during the rest of the year absolutely solitary lives on plantations, the visit to the springs gives the only society of any kind they ever see, and the one chance of showing their clothes and seeing what the other women wear. In short, I do not believe that any one place of summer resort serves so many purposes to any community as the Virginia springs serve to that of the South, and by the springs I mean that circle of mineral waters of various kinds which lie round the White Sulphur, and to which the White Sulphur acts as a kind of distributing reservoir of visitors.

As regards the opinions of the very representative company at the springs on the subject of slavery, it seemed, as well as I could get at it, to be that about one per cent, of the white people regretted the emancipation; but this was composed almost entirely of old persons, who were unable to accommodate themselves to a new order of things, and to whom it meant the loss of personal attendance--perhaps the greatest inconvenience which elderly persons who have been used to valets and maids can undergo. Many such persons at the South were really killed by the social changes produced by the war, as truly as if they had been struck on the battle-field; the bewildered resignation of the survivors is sometimes touching to witness, and the calamity was generally embittered by the wholesale flight of the most trusted household servants, who it was supposed would have despised freedom even if offered in a gold box by Phillips, Garrison, and Greeley in person. Telling one old gentleman who was mourning over the change that the young men to whom I spoke did not agree with him, but thought it an excellent thing, he replied "that those fellows never had known what domestic comfort was"--meaning that their experience did not run back beyond 1865.

The traditions of the old system are, however, unquestionably a better basis for good hotel-keeping than anything we have at the North. The first condition of excellence in all places of entertainment for man and beast is exactingness on the part of the public. To be well cared for you must expect it and be used to it, and this condition the Southerners fulfil in a much higher degree than we do. They look for more attention, and they therefore get it; and the waiter world, partly from habit and partly, no doubt, from race temperament, render it with a cheerfulness we are not familiar with here. But the superiority of manners in all classes is very striking. One rarely meets a man on a Virginia road who does not raise or touch his hat, and this not in a servile way either, but simply as politeness. The bearing of the men toward each other generally, too, has the ineffable charm, which Northern manners are so apt to want, of indicating a recognition of the fact that even if you are no better than any other man, you are different, and that your peculiarities are respectable, and that you are entitled to a certain amount of deference for your private tastes and habits. At the North, on the other hand, manners, even as taught to children, are apt to concede nothing except that you have an immortal soul and a middling chance of salvation, and to avoid anything which is likely to lead you to forget that you are simply a human male.

CHROMO-CIVILIZATION

The last "statement," it is reasonable to hope, has been made in the Beecher-Tilton case previous to the trial at law, and it is safe to say that it has left the public mind in as unsettled a state as ever before. People do not know what to believe, but they do not want to hear any more newspaper discussion by the principal actors. We are not going to attempt any analysis or summing-up of the case at present. It will be time enough to do that after the *dramatis personae* have undergone an examination in court, but we would again warn our readers against looking for any decisive result from the legal trial. The expectations on this point which some of the newspapers and a good many lawyers are encouraging are in the highest degree extravagant. The truth is that only a very small portion of the stuff contained in the various "statements" can, under the rules of evidence, be laid before the jury-

-not, we venture to assert, more than would fill half a newspaper column in all. What *will* be laid before the jury is, in the main, "questions of veracity" between three or four persons whose credit is already greatly shaken, or, in other words, the very kind of questions on which juries are most likely to disagree, even when the jurymen are entirely unprejudiced. In the present case they are sure to be prejudiced, and are sure to be governed, consciously or unconsciously, in reaching their conclusions by agencies wholly foreign to the matter in hand, and are thus very likely to disagree. There are very few men whose opinions about Mr. Beecher's guilt or innocence are not influenced by their own religious and political beliefs, or by their social antecedents or surroundings. A curious and somewhat instructive illustration of the way in which a man's fate in such cases as this may be affected by considerations having no sort of relation to the facts, is afforded by the attitude of the Western press toward the chief actors in the present scandal. It may be said, roughly, that while the press east of the Alleghanies has inclined in Beecher's favor, the newspapers west of them have gone somewhat savagely and persistently against him, and have treated Tilton as a martyr. The cause of such a divergence of views, considering that both Tilton and Beecher are Eastern men, is of course somewhat obscure, but we have no doubt that it is due to a vague feeling prevalent in the West that Tilton's cause is the democratic one--that is, the cause of the poor, friendless man against the rich and successful one--a feeling somewhat like that which in England enlisted the working-classes in London on the side of the Tichborne claimant, in defiance of all reason and evidence, as a poor devil fighting a hard battle with the high and mighty. One of the reporters of a Western paper which has made important contributions to the literature of the scandal, recently accounted for his support of Tilton by declaring that in standing by him he was "fighting the battle of the Bohemians against Capital." Another Western paper, in analyzing the causes of the position taken by the leading New York papers on Beecher's side, ascribed it to the social relations of the editors with him, believing that they met him frequently at dinners and breakfasts, and found him a jovial companion. All this would be laughable enough if it did not show the amount of covert peril--peril against which no precautions can be taken--to which every prominent man's character is exposed. The moment he gets into a scrape of any kind he finds a host of persons whose enmity he never suspected clamoring to have him thrown to the beasts "on general grounds"--that is, in virtue of certain tests adopted by themselves, judged by which, apart from the facts of any particular accusation, a man of his kind is unquestionably a bad fellow. The accusation, in short, furnishes the occasion for destroying him, not necessarily the reason for it.

In Europe there are already abundant signs that the scandal will be considered a symptomatic phenomenon--that is, a phenomenon illustrative of the moral condition of American society generally; for it must not be overlooked that, putting aside altogether the question of Beecher's guilt or innocence, the "statements" furnish sociological revelations of a most singular and instructive kind. The witnesses, in telling their story, although their minds are wholly occupied with the proof or disproof of certain propositions, describe ways of living, standards of right and wrong, traits of manners, codes of propriety, religious and social ideas, which, taken together, form social pictures of great interest and value. Now, if these were really pictures of American society in general, as some European observers are disposed to conclude, we do not hesitate to say that the prospects of the Anglo-Saxon race on this continent would be somewhat gloomy. But we believe we only express the sentiment of all parts of the country when we say that the state of things in Brooklyn revealed by the charges and countercharges has filled the best part of the American people with nearly as much amazement as if an unknown tribe worshipping strange gods had been suddenly discovered on Brooklyn Heights. In fact, the actors in the scandal have the air of persons who are living, not ***more majorum***, by rules with which they are familiar, but like half-civilized people who have got hold of a code which they do not understand, and the phrases of which they use without being able to adapt their conduct to it.

We have not space at our command to illustrate this as fully as we could wish, even if the patience of our readers would permit of it, but we can perhaps illustrate sufficiently within a very short compass. We have already spoken of the Oriental extravagance of the language used in the scandal, which might pass in Persia or Central Arabia, where wild hyperbole is permitted by the genius of the language, and where people are accustomed to it in conversation, understand it perfectly, and make unconscious allowance for it. Displayed here in the United States, in a mercantile community, and in a tongue characterized by directness and simplicity, it makes the actors almost entirely incomprehensible to people outside their own set, as is shown by the attempts made to explain and understand the letters in the case. Most of the critics, both the friendly and hostile, are compelled to treat them as written in a sort of dialect which has to be read with the aid of commentary, glosses, and parallels, and accompanied, like the study of Homer or the Reg-Veda, by a careful examination of the surroundings of the writers, the conditions of their birth and education, the usages of the circle in which they live, and the social and religious influences by which they have been moulded, and so on. Their almost entire want of any sense of necessary connection between facts and written statements has been strikingly revealed by Moulton's production of various drafts or outlines of cards, reports, and letters which the actors proposed from time to time to get up and publish for the purpose of settling their troubles and warding off exposure by imposing on the public. No savages could have acted with a more simple-minded unconsciousness of truth. Moulton, according to his own story, helped Beecher to publish a lying card; got Tilton to procure from his wife a lying letter; and Tilton concocted a lying report for the committee, in which he made them express the highest admiration for himself, his adulterous wife, and her paramour. Here we have a bit of the machinery of high civilization--a committee, with its investigation and report, used, or attempted to be used, with just the kind of savage directness with which a Bongo would use it, when once he came to understand it, and found he could make it serve some end, and with just as little reference to the moral aspect of the transaction.

Take, again, Tilton's account of the motives which governed him in his treatment of his wife and of Beecher. He is evidently aware that there are two codes regulating a man's conduct under such circumstances--one the Christian code and the other the conventional code of honor, or, as he calls it, "club-house morality"; but it soon became clear that he had no distinct conception of their difference. Having been brought up under the Christian code, and taught, doubtless, to regard the term "gentleman" as a name for a heartless epicurean, he started off by forgiving both Beecher and his wife, or, as the lawyers say, condoning their offence; and he speaks scornfully of the religious ignorance of the committee in assuming in their report that there was any offence for which a Christian was not bound to accept an apology as a sufficient atonement. The club-house code would, however, have prescribed the infliction of vengeance on Beecher by exposing him. Accordingly, Tilton mixes the two codes up in the most absurd way. Having, as a Christian, forgiven Beecher, he began, thirty days after the discovery of the offence, to expose him as a "gentleman," and kept forgiving and exposing him continuously through the whole four years, the *eclat* of such a relation to Beecher having evidently an irresistible temptation for him. Finally, when Dr. Bacon called him a "dog," he threw aside the Christian *role* altogether and began assailing his enemy with truly heathen virulence and vigor. A more curious blending of two conceptions of duty is not often seen, and it was doubtless due to the fact that no system of training or culture had made any impression on the man or gone more than skin deep. His interview with Beecher, too, by appointment, at his own house, for the purpose of ascertaining by a comparison of dates and reference to his wife's diary the probable paternity of her youngest child, which he describes with the utmost simplicity, is, we venture to say, an incident absolutely without precedent, and one which may safely be pronounced foreign to our civilization. Whether it really occurred, or Tilton invented it, it makes him a problem in social philosophy of considerable interest.

Moulton's story, too, furnishes several puzzles of the same kind. That an English-speaking Protestant married couple in easy circumstances and of fair education, and belonging to a religious circle, should not only be aware that their pastor was a libertine and should be keeping it a secret for him, but should make his adulteries the subject of conversation with him in the family circle, is hardly capable of explanation by reference to any known and acknowledged tendency of our society. But perhaps the most striking thing in Moulton's *role* is that while he appears on the scene as a gentleman or "man of the world," who does for honor's sake what the other actors do from fear of God, his whole course is a kind of caricature of what a gentleman under like circumstances would really do. For instance, he accepts Beecher's confidence, which may have been unavoidable, and betrays it by telling various people, from time to time, of the several incidents of Beecher's trouble, which is something of which a weak or loose-tongued person--vain of the task in which he was engaged, as it seemed to him, *i.e.*, of keeping the peace between two great men--might readily be guilty. But he tells the public of it in perfect unconsciousness that there was anything discreditable in it, as he does of his participation in the writing of lying letters and cards, and his passing money over from the adulterer to pacify the injured husband. In fact, he carries, according to his own account, his services to Beecher to a point at which it is very difficult to distinguish them from those of a pander, maintaining at the same time relations of the most disgusting confidence with Mrs. Tilton. Finally, too, when greatly perplexed as to his course, he goes publicly and with *eclat* for advice to a lawyer, with whom no gentleman, in the proper sense of the term, could maintain intimate personal relation or safely consult on a question of honor. The moral insensibility shown in his visit to General Butler is one of the strange parts of the affairs.

We have, of course, only indicated in the briefest way some of the things which may be regarded as symptomatic of strange mental and moral conditions in the circle in which the affair has occurred. The explanation of them in any way that would generally be considered satisfactory would be a difficult task. The influences which bring about a certain state of manners at any given time or place are always numerous and generally obscure, but we think something of this sort may be safely offered in consideration of the late "goings on" in Brooklyn.

In the first place, the newspapers and other cheap periodicals, and the lyceum lectures and small colleges, have diffused through the community a kind of smattering of all sorts of knowledge, a taste for reading and for "art"--that is, a desire to see and own pictures-- which, taken together, pass with a large body of slenderly equipped persons as "culture," and give them an unprecedented self-confidence in dealing with all the problems of life, and raise them in their own minds to a plane on which they see nothing higher, greater, or better than themselves. Now, culture, in the only correct and safe sense of the term, is the result of a process of discipline, both mental and moral. It is not a thing that can be picked up, or that can be got by doing what one pleases. It cannot be acquired by desultory reading, for instance, or travelling in Europe. It comes of the protracted exercise of the faculties for given ends, under restraints of some kind, whether imposed by one's self or other people. In fact, it might not improperly be called the art of doing easily what you don't like to do. It is the breaking-in of the powers to the service of the will; and a man who has got it is not simply a person who knows a good deal, for he may know very little, but a man who has obtained an accurate estimate of his own capacity, and of that of his fellows and predecessors, who is aware of the nature and extent of his relations to the world about him, and who is at the same time capable of using his powers to the best advantage. In short, the man of culture is the man who has formed his ideals through labor and self-denial. To be real, therefore, culture ought to affect a man's whole character and not merely store his memory with facts. Let us add, too, that it may be got in various ways, through home influences as well as through schools or colleges; through living in a highly organized society, making imperious demands on one's time and faculties, as well as through the restraints of a severe course of study. A good deal of it was obtained from the old Calvinistic theology, against which, in the days of its predominance, the most bumptious youth hit his head at an early period of his career, and was reduced to thoughtfulness and self-examination, and forced to walk in ways that were not always to his liking.

If all this be true, the mischievous effects of the pseudo-culture of which we have spoken above may be readily estimated. A society of ignoramuses who know they are ignoramuses might lead a tolerably happy and useful existence, but a society of ignoramuses each of whom thinks he is a Solon would be an approach to Bedlam let loose, and something analogous to this may really be seen to-day in some parts of this country. A large body of persons has arisen, under the influence of the common schools, magazines, newspapers, and the rapid acquisition of wealth, who are not only engaged in enjoying themselves after their fashion, but who firmly believe that they have reached, in the matter of social, mental, and moral culture, all that is attainable or desirable by anybody, and who, therefore, tackle all the problems of the day--men's, women's, and children's rights and duties, marriage, education, suffrage, life, death, and immortality--with supreme indifference to what anybody else thinks or has ever thought, and have their own trumpery prophets, prophetesses, heroes and heroines, poets, orators, scholars and philosophers, whom they worship with a kind of barbaric fervor. The result is a kind of mental and moral chaos, in which many of the fundamental rules of living, which have been worked out painfully by thousands of years of bitter human experience, seem in imminent risk of disappearing totally.

Now, if we said that a specimen of this society had been unearthed in Brooklyn by the recent exposures, we should, doubtless to many people, seem to say a very hard thing, and yet this, with the allowances and reservations which have of course to be made for all attempts to describe anything so vague and fleeting as a social state, is what we do mean to say. That Mr. Beecher's preaching, falling on such a mass of disorder, should not have had a more purifying and organizing effect, is due, we think, to the absence from it of anything in the smallest degree disciplinary, either in the shape of systematic theology, with its tests and standards, or of a social code, with its pains and penalties. What he has most encouraged, if we may judge by some of the fruits, is vague aspiration and lachrymose sensibility. The ability to dare and do, the readiness to ask one's due which comes of readiness to render their due to others, the profound consciousness of the need of sound habits to brace and fortify morals, which are the only true foundation and support of a healthy civilization, are things which he either has not preached or which his preaching has only stifled.

"THE SHORT-HAIRS" AND "THE SWALLOW-TAILS"

There is a story afloat that Mr. John Morrissey made his appearance, one day during the past week, in Madison Square, in full evening dress, including white gloves and cravat, and bearing a French dictionary under his arm, and that, being questioned by his friends as to the object of this display, he replied that he was going to see Major Wickham and ask him for an office in the only costume in which such an application would have a chance of success. In other words, he was acting what over in Brooklyn would be called "an allegory," and which was intended to expose in a severe and telling way the Mayor's gross partiality, in the use of his patronage, for the well-dressed and well-educated members of society--a partiality which Mr. Morrissey and his party consider not only unfair but ridiculous. This demonstration, too, was one of the few indications which have as yet met the public eye of a very real division of the Democratic party in this city into two sets of politicians, known familiarly as "Short-Hairs" and "Swallow-Tails"--the former comprising the rank and file of the voters and the latter "the property-owners and substantial men," who are endeavoring to make Tammany an instrument of reform and to manage the city in the interest of the taxpayers. Mayor Wickham belongs, it is said, to the latter class, and has given, it seems, in the eyes of the former, some proofs of a desire to reserve responsible offices for persons of some pretensions to gentility, and exhibited some disfavor for the selections of the "workers" in the various wards.

But we do not undertake to describe with accuracy the origin or nature of the split; all we know is that the Short-Hairs are disgusted, and that their hostility to the Swallow-Tails is very bitter, and that when Mr. Morrissey proclaimed, in the manner we have described, that a man needed to wear evening dress and to know French in order to get a place, he gave feeble expression to the rage of the masses. They have, too, concocted an arrangement which embodies their idea of a well-administered government, and which consists in compelling the departments to spend in wages in each district at least $1.50 for each Democratic vote cast, and to apportion the appropriations with strict reference to this rule, the money, of course, to go to the nominees of Democratic politicians. The plan departs from that of the French national workshops in that it discriminates between laborers, but in other respects it has all the characteristics of well-developed Communism. The way to meet it, according to our venerable contemporary, the *Evening Post*, is to have the taxpayers point out to the voters who are to receive the money that they (the taxpayers) cannot well spare it, that they need it for their own use, and that this mode of administering corporate funds is condemned by all the leading writers on government. The Swallow-Tails know so well, however, with what howls of mingled mirth and indignation the Short-Hairs would receive such suggestions that they never make them, but content themselves with confining the distribution of the money to the members of their own division quietly and unostentatiously, as far as lies in their power, which, we candidly confess, we do not think is very far.

It would be doing the Short-Hairs injustice, however, if we allowed the reader to remain under the impression that the unwillingness to have the Swallow-Tails monopolize or even have a share of the office was peculiar to them, or that John Morrissey's protest would be unintelligible anywhere out of New York. On the contrary, when he started out with his French dictionary he was giving expression to a feeling which is to be found in greater or less intensity in every State in the Union. The great division of politicians into Short-Hairs and Swallow-Tails is not confined to this city. It is found in every city in the country in which there is much diversity of condition among the inhabitants. Nor did Morrissey mean simply to protest against training as a qualification for the work of administration, as the *Tribune* assumed in a sharp and incisive lecture which it read him the other day. We doubt if any pugilist in his secret heart despises training. He knows how much depends on it, and as he is not apt to possess much discriminating power, he is not likely to mark off any particular class of work as not needing it. What the Short-Hairs dislike in the Swallow-Tails is the feeling of personal superiority which they imagine them to entertain, and which they think finds a certain expression in careful dressing and in the possession of certain accomplishments. In fact, the Swallow-Tails whom the New York rough detests and would like to keep out of public life, belong to the class known in Massachusetts as the "White-cravat-and-daily-bath gentlemen," and which is there just as unpopular as here, and has even greater difficulty in getting office there than here.

The line of division in New York is, however, drawn much lower down. The Massachusetts Short-Hair is a man of intelligence, of some education, who wears a plain black neglige and rumpled shirt-front and soft hat, and disregards the condition of his nails, and takes a warm bath occasionally. The New Yorker, on the other hand, wears such clothes as he can get, and only bathes in the hot weather and off the public wharf. If he has good luck and makes money, either in the public service or otherwise, he displays it not in any richness in his toilet or in greater care of his person, but in the splendor of his jewels. One of his first purchases is a diamond-pin, which he sticks in his shirt-front, but he never sees any connection of an aesthetic kind between the linen and the pin, and will wear the latter in a very dirty shirt-front as cheerfully as in a clean one--in fact, more cheerfully, as he has a vague feeling that by showing it he atones for or excuses the condition of the linen. In fact, the Short-Hair view of dress would be found on examination to be, in nearly ninety-nine cases out of a hundred, something of this kind: that the constant care of the person which produces an impression of neatness and appropriateness, and makes a man look "genteel," is the expression of a certain state of mind; that a man would not take so much trouble to make himself look different from the ordinary run of people whom he meets, unless he thought himself in some way superior to them, or, in other words, thought himself a "gentleman" and them common fellows, and that he therefore fairly deserves the hatred of those of whom he thus openly parades his contempt.

A New York Short-Hair seldom goes farther than this in his speculations, though he doubtless has also a vague idea that a well-dressed man is not so likely to stand by his friends in politics as a more careless one. In New England, as might be expected, however, the popular dislike of that "culte de la personne," as some Frenchman has called it, which distinguishes "the white-cravat-and-daily-bath gentleman," has provided itself with a moral basis. There is there a strong presumption that the Swallow-Tail is a frivolous person, who bestows on his tailoring, and his linen, and his bathing, and his manners the time and attention which the Short-Hair or "plain blunt man" reserves for reflection on the graver concerns of life, and especially on the elevation of his fellow-men, and this presumption even a career of philanthropy and the composition of the "Principia" would not in many minds suffice to overthrow. We believe it is authentic that General Grant never got over the impression produced on him by seeing that Mr. Motley parted his hair in the middle, and it is said--and if not true is not unlikely,--that Mr. R. H. Dana's practice of wearing kid gloves told heavily against him in his memorable contest with Butler in the Essex district. We may all remember, too, the gigantic efforts made by Mr. Sumner and others in Congress to have our representatives abroad prohibited from wearing court-dress. What dress they wore was of course, *per se*, a matter of no consequence, provided it was not immodest. The fervor on the subject was due to the deeply rooted feeling that even the amount of care for externals exhibited in putting on an embroidered coat or knee-breeches indicated a light-mindedness against the very appearance of which the minister of a republic ought to guard carefully. It is partly to produce the effect of seriousness of purpose, but mainly to avoid the appearance of airs of social or mental superiority, that nearly all skilful politicians dress with elaborate negligence. In most country districts no complaints can be made of men in office such as the New York Short-Hair makes against the Swallow-Tail. They fling on their easy-fitting black clothes in a way that leaves them their whole time for the study of public affairs and attention to the wants of their constituents, and at the same time recalls their humble beginnings.

What strikes one, however, as most curious in the controversy between the Short-Hairs and the Swallow-Tails is the illustration it affords of the rigidity with which every class or grade in civilization treats its own social conventions, whatever they may be, as final, and as having some subtle but necessary connection with morals. When the Indian squats round the tribal pot in his breech-clout, and eats his dinner with his dirty paw, he is fully satisfied that he is as well equipped, both as regards dress and manners, not only as a man need be, but as a man ought to be. The toilet, the chamber, and the dinner-table of a plain New England farmer he treats as wasteful and ridiculous excess, and if good for anything, good only for plunder. The farmer, on the other hand, loathes the Indian and his ways, and thinks him a filthy beast, and that he (the farmer) has reached the limits of the proper as regards clothes and food and personal habits, and that the city man who puts greater elaboration into his life is a fribble, who is to be pitied, if not despised and distrusted. In short, we can hardly go one step into the controversy without coming on the old question, What are luxuries and what necessities? and, as usual, the majority decides it in the manner that best suits itself. It may be said without exaggeration that the progress of civilization has consisted largely in the raising of what is called "the standard of living," or, in other words, the multiplication of the things deemed necessary for personal comfort, and, as this raising of the standard has always been begun by the few, the many have always fought against it as a sign of selfishness or affectation until they themselves were able to adopt it.

The history of the bath furnishes a curious though tolerably familiar illustration of this. The practice of bathing disappeared from Western Europe with the fall of the Roman Empire. The barbarians were themselves dirty fellows, like the Indians, and their descendants remained dirty in spite of the growth of civilization among them, putting their money, like the Short-Hair, mainly into jewels and other ornaments. As long as linen was scarce and dear, changes were, of course, seldom made, and the odor of even "the best society" was so insupportable that perfumes had to be lavishly used to overcome it. The increased cheapness of linen and more recently of cotton, and the increased facilities for bathing, have in our own day made personal cleanliness a common virtue; but an occasional bath is still as much as is thought, through the greater part of the world, compatible with moral earnestness and high aims. Of late, indeed within the memory of the present generation, persons mainly belonging to the wealthier class in England have boldly begun to bathe every day, and they have finally succeeded in establishing the rule that a gentleman is bound to bathe, or "tub," as they call it, every day, and that the usage cannot be persistently neglected without loss of position. Indeed, there are few social casuists in England who would decide, without great hesitation and anxiety, that any English-speaking man was a gentleman who did not take a daily bath. That this view of the matter should be accepted by the great body of those who would rather not bathe every day is not to be expected, nor is it to be wondered at that they should consider it offensive, and that the practice of sponging one's self in cold water every morning should in caucuses be looked on as a disqualification for political life. There is, of course, a necessary and provoking, though tacit, assumption of superiority in the display of greater cleanliness than other people show, just as there is in coming into a room and finding fault with the closeness of the air in which other people are sitting comfortably. It is tantamount to saying that what is good enough for them is not good enough for you, and they always either openly or secretly resent it.

The popular distrust of the practice of wearing white cravats in the evening may be traced to the same causes. The savage makes no change of toilet for the evening. He dresses for war and religious ceremonies, but he goes to a social reunion or feast in such clothes as he happens to have on when the invitation finds him. The plain man of civilized life, under similar circumstances, puts on a clean shirt and his best suit of clothes. This suit, among the European peasantry, is apt to be of simply the same cut and material as the working suit, or, as it would be called in Brooklyn, "the garb of toil." Among Americans, it is a black suit, like that of a clergyman, and includes a silk cravat, generally black, but permissibly colored. The whole matter is, however, one of pure convention. Now, it has been found of late years a matter of convenience, and of great convenience especially to hard-worked men and men of moderate means who are exposed to the constant social demands of the great cities of the world, to have a costume in which one can appear on any festive occasion, great or small, which all, gentle or simple, are alike expected to wear, which is neither rich nor gaudy, and in which every man may feel sure that he is properly dressed; and the dress fixed on for this purpose now throughout the civilized world is the plain suit of black, with the swallow-tailed coat, commonly called "evening dress."

Nothing can be simpler or less pretentious, or more democratic. Nobody can add anything to it or take anything away from it. Many attempts to modify it have been made during the last thirty years by leaders of fashion, and they have all failed, because it meets one of the great wants of human nature. It is only within the last fifteen years that it has obtained a firm foothold in American cities. People looked on it with suspicion, as a sign of some inward and spiritual naughtiness, and regarded the frock-coat with its full skirts as the only garment in which a serious-minded man, with a proper sense of his origin and destiny, and correct feelings about popular government, could make his appearance in a lady's parlor. Why, nobody could tell, for there was a time, not very far back, when the frock-coat was itself an innovation. Of late--that is, within, perhaps, twenty years--the Swallow-Tails of the world have exchanged the black or colored for a white cravat, and justify themselves by saying that it not only looks cleaner, but is cleaner of necessity than a silk one, and that you cannot look too clean or fresh about your throat when you present yourself in a lady's house on a festive occasion. Nevertheless, the plain, blunt men are not satisfied. They do not as yet feel sure as to its meaning. They think it indicates either over-thoughtfulness about trifles or else a leaning, slight though it be, toward despotism and free-trade. They will now all, or nearly all, wear evening dress with a black cravat, but even those of them who will consent to put on a white one do so with a certain shamefacedness and sense of backsliding, and of treachery to some good cause, though they do not exactly know which.

JUDGES AND WITNESSES

The proceedings in the recent Bravo poisoning case have raised a good deal of discussion in England as to the license of counsel in cross-examination--a question which recent trials in this country have shown to possess no little interest for us also. In the Bravo inquest, as in the Tichborne case and the Beecher trial of the last year, the cross-examination of the witnesses was pushed into matters very remotely connected with the issue under trial, so that the general result of the inquiry was not, as in most cases, the eliciting of a certain number of facts bearing on the question in court, but a complete revelation of the whole private life of a family, or of a certain part of it, and even of a whole circle of families. The glaring exposure of matters usually kept close, and not even talked about, formed in fact the great fascination of these *causes celebres*. It was difficult at the first blush to see how in the Beecher trial Tilton's eccentric nocturnal habits could have thrown any light upon the question of Beecher's guilt; nor in the Tichborne case was it at all apparent that an answer to the inquiry put to some witness--whether he had, at some distant period of time, had improper relations with some persons not connected with the case--could even remotely tend to settle the claimant's identity. The *Pall Mall Gazette*, discussing this kind of cross-examination resorted to for the purpose of breaking down the credit of a witness--of "showing him up" to the jury, and thus inducing them to pay less attention to his evidence than they otherwise would--has stated the case in the following manner: "Suppose, it says, that the legislature of a free country were some fine morning to pass a law authorizing anyone who chose to take it into his head to compel any inhabitant of the country to answer any questions he might think fit to put with regards to the other's moral character, his relations with his parents, brothers and sisters, wife and children, his business affairs, his property, his debts, and in fact his whole private life, and to do all this without there being any dispute between them or even any alleged grievance, what would be thought of such a law? Would it be endured for an instant?" Now, this, the *Pall Mall Gazette* continues, is to-day the law of England. It is just to this odious tyranny which anyone, by bringing a suit, can, under the vague and almost unlimited power to punish for "contempt of court," force submission.

The law on this subject is, generally speaking, the same in the United States as in England, and this tyranny, if it really exists, weighs upon us as heavily as it does upon Englishmen. The first question that suggests itself is whether this is really a fair statement of law, and, of course, the *Pall Mall Gazette* admits that there exist limitations of the right of cross-examination, but it contends that these are so undefined as to amount to little or nothing in the way of protection. The authorities contain little on the subject, except that cross-examination as to credit is allowed to go very far, and that judges may in their discretion stop it when it goes too far. But judicial discretion is proverbially an uncertain thing. It varies not merely with the court, but even in the same judge it is affected by the state of his temper, his curiosity, his feeling toward the counsel who is examining, and by thousands of other things that no one can know anything about or depend upon. Usually it is easier not to exercise than to exercise discretion, and the result is that the right of cross-examination is usually unchecked, and in most important cases which are widely reported the right is pushed to lengths which, with witnesses of any sensibility, amount to a process of slow torture. If the right is abused in England, it is unquestionably abused here, and probably at the time of the Beecher trial we should have had complaints about it but for the fact that in the singular society in which the parties to that case lives, a craving for notoriety had been developed which made any discussion of their private affairs less disagreeable than it is to most people. But with the great majority of mankind there is nothing more odious than the extraction, by a sharp, hostile lawyer, from their own unwilling lips, of the details of their moral history. There is probably no one in existence, however good, and however quiet his conscience may be, who can endure without a shudder the thought of every transaction of his past life being dragged out in a court of justice for the amusement of a gaping crowd. Exactly how far the right is abused, and how far the discretionary powers of courts to limit its abuse accomplish their end, it is impossible to say, for it is only in sporadic cases of unusual importance that interest in the result is strong enough to warrant a lawyer's going to great length in cross-examination. Usually, too, it should be said for the credit of the profession, reputable lawyers shrink from outraging a witness's sensibility. But after everything is admitted that can be admitted in favor of the existing state of the law, it is impossible to deny that the door is left very wide open to disgraceful assaults upon credit which inflict serious and irreparable damage.

The difficulty is not in pointing out the evil, which is plain enough, but in suggesting a remedy. The right of cross-examination is one of the most important instruments provided by the machinery of our law for the discovery of facts, and on the credibility of witnesses all cases hinge. The moment we begin to limit it by fixed rules we enter on dangerous ground. It might seem as if the solution of the problem lay in the enactment of a rule that witnesses should only be cross-examined as to their general reputation with regard to truth, and as to the matters involved in the case directly affecting their credibility; but this would by no means do. Suppose, for instance, that the suit is a common action for the purchase-money of a piece of cloth, and the defendant brings a witness who swears that he saw the defendant pay the money to the plaintiff, while the plaintiff has only his own evidence to rely upon in proof of non-payment; if, in such case, the plaintiff were merely allowed to cross-examine the witness directly, he would in all probability lose the case. The testimony would be two to one against him, and the story of the witness as the only disinterested person would probably be believed by the jury. But suppose that, on cross-examination, it turns out that this witness can give no good account of his manner of earning his living or of his place of residence; that he had been arrested not long before as a vagrant, and that down to the time of the action he had no respectable clothes, and that he suddenly became possessed of some; that he deserted from the army immediately after getting his bounty-money, and so on, there can be little doubt that his credit with the jury would be much impaired, and justly so, although no direct evidence of his being a perjurer had been introduced, and not a particle of his testimony had been strictly controverted. Everyone who has followed with any care the evidence taken in celebrated murder trials or divorce cases knows how frequently a rigid cross-examination lays bare motives and prejudices on the part of witnesses which, often without their knowing it themselves, tend to bias their account of facts.

The problem, therefore, is to devise some means by which these benefits of a searching cross-examination may be retained and yet the abuse got rid of. The only feasible way of meeting the difficulty yet proposed is that of drawing up a series of rules or general directions as to evidence which shall not attempt to prescribe formal limits for cross-examination, but shall lay down in explicit words the general principles which should govern a judge in such cases. These rules would practically be a definition of the "discretion" he is now supposed to exercise. They would, for example, direct him not to allow an examination into matters so remote in time from the case in hand that they can have no bearing on the credibility of the witness; not to allow questions to be put which are plainly malicious and asked for the purpose of irritating the witness; and not to allow any examination into transactions which, though they may have a bearing on the character of a witness, have none on his credibility, *e.g.*, an inquiry, in a murder case, of a witness in good standing, as to domestic difficulties with a deceased wife. It is not easy to lay down beforehand any rules by which we can discriminate the kind of evidence as to transactions involving moral character which ought not to affect credibility, but every one can easily imagine instances of such evidence. General directions of the kind we have just suggested are no more than a formal enunciation of the manner in which the "discretion" of a good judge would be and is exercised. They do not change the law, but they remind judges of what they may forget, and they may be appealed to by a persecuted witness with far more certainty than judicial "discretion." In the Indian Code, which is probably the best body of law that the legal reform movement begun by Bentham in the last century has yet produced, rules of this kind have been laid down, and we believe have been found to work with success.

"THE DEBTOR CLASS"

A Washington correspondent, describing, the other day, the motives which animated the majority in Congress in its performances on the currency question, said, and we believe truly, that most of the inflationists in that body knew very well what the evils of paper-money were, so that argument on that point was wasted on them. But they knew also that large issues of irredeemable paper would make it easier for debtors to pay off their creditors, and came to the conclusion that as the number of debtors in the country was greater than the number of creditors, it was wise policy for a politician to curry favor with the former by helping them to cheat the persons who had lent them money or sold them goods. This explanation of the conduct of the majority may be a startling and sad one, but that it is highly probable nobody can deny. All the debates help to confirm it. In every speech, made either in opposition to resumption or in favor of inflation, a portion of the community known as "the debtor class" has appeared as the object of the orator's tenderest solicitude. The great reason for not returning to specie payments hitherto has been the fear that contraction would press hard on "the debtor class;" it is for "the debtor class" we need more paper "*per capita*;" and indeed, no matter what proposal we make in the direction of financial reform, we are met by pictures of the frightful effects which will be produced by it on the "debtor class." Moreover, in listening to its champions, a foreigner might conclude that in America debtors either all live together in a particular part of the country, or worse, a particular costume, like mediaeval Jews, and are divided from the rest of the community by tastes and habits, so that it would be proper for an American to put "debtor" or "creditor" on his card as a description of his social status. He might, too, not unnaturally begin to mourn over the negligence of the framers of the Constitution in not recognizing this marked distribution of American society. Truly, he would say, the debtors ought to have representatives in the Senate and House to look after their special interests; these unfortunate and helpless men ought not to be left to the charitable care of volunteers like Messrs. Morton, and Logan, and Kelly. The great sham and pretence with which America has so long tried to impose on Europe, that there were no classes in the United States, ought at last to be formally swept away, and proper legal provision made for the protection of a body of men which has been in all ages the object of atrocious oppression, and seems in America, strange to say, to constitute the larger portion of the community. In travelling through the country, too, he would be constantly on the lookout for the debtors. He would ask in the cities for the "debtors' quarter," and when introduced to a gentleman in the cars or in the hotels, would inquire privately whether he was a debtor or a creditor, so as to avoid hurting his feelings by indiscreet allusion to specie or contraction. His amazement would be very great on learning that there was no way of telling whether an American citizen was either debtor or creditor; that the "debtor class" was not to be found, as such, in any part of the country, or, indeed, anywhere but in the brains of the Logans and Mortons, and was introduced into the debates simply as a John Doe or Richard Roe, to give a little vividness to the speaker's railings against property.

Now, as in every civilized society, the vast majority of the population of this country are in debt, to some slight degree. It is only paupers, criminals, and lunatics who owe absolutely nothing. The day-laborer is pretty sure to have a small bill at the grocer's, and all his neighbors, in the ascending grades of commercial respectability, no matter how prompt and accurate they may be in the discharge of their obligations, are sure to owe the butcher and baker and milkman a greater or less amount. In fact the conduct of life on a cash basis would be impossible or intolerable. Of course, too, there are scattered all over the country men who owe a great deal of money and to whom little is due, and whose interest it would be to have the coinage adulterated. But then the number of these persons is very small, and they are mostly great speculators, who pass for rich men, and whose interests Congress is in reality not in the least desirous of protecting. Poor men, as a rule, are hardly ever greatly in debt, because nobody will trust them. We suspect that the number of those in this city who could borrow fifty dollars without security would not be found to be over one-twentieth of the population. The persons to whom loans are made by banks, insurance companies, and other institutions are almost all men of wealth or men who have the conduct of great enterprises, and do not need legislation to help them to take care of themselves. They are great merchants, or manufacturers, or brokers, or contractors, or railroad-builders. In fact, in so far as the debtors can be called a class, they form a very small class, and a class of remarkable shrewdness and of enormous power, over whom it is ludicrous for the Government to exercise a fatherly care.

The bulk of the population in this, as in every moderately prosperous community in the western world is composed of creditors. The creditor class, in other words, contains the great body of the American people, and any legislation intended to enable debtors to cheat is aimed at nineteen-twentieths, at the very least, of American citizens. Any mail who remains very long in the position of a debtor simply, and acquires no footing as a creditor, disappears from the surface of society. Bankruptcy or the house of correction is pretty sure to overtake him. It would be well-nigh impossible in this large city or in any other to find a man who had no pecuniary claims on someone else. The humblest hod-carrier becomes a creditor every day after making his first ascent of the ladder, and remains so until Saturday night, and continually replaces himself in "the creditor class," as long as life and health remain to him; and the same phenomenon presents itself in all fields of industry. Every sewing-girl and maid-servant is looking forward to a payment of earned money, and has the strongest interest in knowing for certain what its purchasing power will be.

All depositors in savings-banks, and their number in New York City is greater than that of the voters, belong to the creditor class; all holders of policies of insurances, all owners of government bonds and State and bank stocks, belong to it also. The Western farmers and house-owners who have borrowed money at the East on bond and mortgage, who probably make as near an approach to a debtor class as any other body or persons in the community, and whom Congressional demagogues probably hoped to serve by enabling them to outwit their creditors, even these are not simply or mainly debtors. Any man who is carrying on his business with borrowed money, on which he pays eight or ten per cent., must be every week putting other people in debt to him or he would speedily be ruined. The means of paying those who have trusted him is acquired by his trusting others. Either he is selling goods on credit, or entering into contracts, or rendering services which give him the position of a creditor, and make it of the last importance to him that the value of money and the state of the public mind about money should not be materially different six months hence from what they are now.

Of course there is more than one way of defining the term "self-interest." There is one sense in which it is used by children, savages, and thieves, and which makes it mean immediate gratification, and this appears to be the sense in which it is used by the inflationists in Congress, in considering what is for the good of those Western men who owe money at the East. In that sense, it is a good thing for a man to lie, cheat, steal, and embezzle whenever it shall appear that by so doing he will satisfy his appetites or put money in his pockets. But civilized and commercial, to say nothing of Christian, society is founded on the theory that men look forward and expect to carry on business for several years, and to lay up money for their old age, and establish their children in life, and that they recognize the necessity of self-restraint and loyalty to engagements. The doctrines, on the other hand, which are preached in Congress about the best mode of dealing with debts--that is, with other people's money--have never before been heard in a civilized legislature, or anywhere outside of a council of buccaneers, and, if acted on by the community, would produce anarchy. The fact that Morton and Butler, who preach them and get them embodied in forms of words called "acts," are legislators, disguises, but ought not to disguise, the other fact, that these two men are simply playing the part of receivers or "fences." There probably never was a more striking illustration of the immorality in which, as it was long ago remarked, any principle of government is sure to land people if pushed to its last extreme, than the theory which is now urged on our attention--that superiority of numbers will justify fraud; or, in other words, that if the number of those who borrow should happen to be greater than the number of those who lend, "a vote" is all that is needed to wipe out the debts, either openly or by payment in bits of paper or pebbles. Of course, the converse of this would also be true--that if the lenders were in a majority, they would be justified in reducing the debtors to slavery. If the question of humanity or brotherhood were raised as an objection, that, too, could be settled by a ballot. We laugh at the poor African who consults his wooden fetish before he takes any step in the business of his wretched and darkened life; but when a Caucasian demagogue tries to show us that the springs of justice and truth are to be found in a comparison of ten thousand bits of paper with nine thousand similar bits, we listen with gravity, and are half inclined to believe that there is something in it.

COMMENCEMENT ADMONITION

It is quite evident that with, the multiplication of colleges, which is very rapid, it will, before long, become impossible for the newspapers to furnish the reports of the proceedings in and about commencement which they now lay before their readers with such profuseness. The long letters describing with wearisome minuteness what has been described already fifty times will undoubtedly before long be given up. So also, we fancy, will the reports of the "baccalaureate sermons," if these addresses are to retain their value as pieces of parting advice to young men. There is nothing in the newspaper literature, on the whole, less edifying, and sometimes more amusing, than the reporter's ***precis*** of pulpit discourses, so thoroughly does he deprive them of force find vigor and point, and often of intelligibility. The ordinary sermon addressed on Sunday to the ordinary congregation deals with a great variety of topics, and from many different points of view, and with more or less diversity of method. The baccalaureate sermon, on the other hand, consists, from the necessity of the case, in the main of advice to youths at their entrance on life, and the substance of such discourses can, in the nature of things, undergo no great change from year to year, and must be strikingly similar in all the colleges. Any freshness they may have they must owe to the rhetorical powers of particular preachers, and even these cannot greatly vary in dealing with so familiar a theme. What the old man has to say to the young man, the teacher to the pupil, the father to the son, at the moment when the gates of the great world are flung open to the college graduate, has undergone but little modification in a thousand years, and has become very well known to all collegians long before they take their degree. To make the parting words of warning and encouragement tell on ears that are now eager for other and louder sounds, everything that can be done needs to be done to preserve their freshness and their pathos, and certainly nothing could do as much to deprive them of both one and the other as hashing them up annually in a slovenly report as part of the news of the day.

It is not, however, the advice contained in baccalaureate sermons, but all advice to young men, that needs in our time to be dealt out with greater circumspection and economy. Authority has within the last hundred or even fifty years undergone a serious loss of power, and this loss of power has shown itself nowhere more markedly than in the work of education. It has indeed almost completely changed the relation of parents and children, and teachers and scholars, so that it is now almost as necessary to prove the reasonableness and utility of any course of action which is required of boys as of mature men. Persuasion has, in other words, taken the place of command, and there is nobody left whose dictum owes much of its weight to his years or his office. Boys as well as their elders now expect advice to be based on personal experience, and do not listen with any great seriousness or deference to admonitions the value of which the utterer has not himself personally tested.

It follows, therefore, that the persons whom the young men of our time hear most readily on the conduct of life are those who have had practical acquaintance with the difficulties of living up to the ideals which are so eloquently painted in the college chapel, and who have found out in their own persons what it costs to be pure and upright, and faithful and industrious, and persistent in the struggle that goes on in the various callings which lie outside the college walls. For this reason, probably, no addresses at commencement have the value of those which are delivered now and then by men who have come back for a brief day to tell the next generation of the way life looks to those who for years have been wrestling with its problems, and have had actual experience of the virtues and defects of that early equipment and training on which such enormous sums are now spent in this country. The more advice from this quarter young men get the better. Nobody can talk so effectively to them at the moment when they are about to face the world on their own responsibility as the lawyers and merchants and ministers and politicians who have been facing it for twenty-five or thirty years with all the outward signs of success. If it were possible for every college in the country to get one such man at commencement whose powers of expression would do justice to his experience, and who for this one day in the year would without fear or favor tell what he thought about success and about the conditions of success--about the kind of troubles which beset men in the callings with which he is most familiar--we should probably soon have a body of advice so impressive and fruitful that it would serve the needs and excite the interest of more than one generation. The young have been told to be good until they have grown weary of hearing it, particularly as it is always represented to them as a comparatively simple matter, and when they go out in the world and find what a hard and complex thing duty is they are very apt to look back to the ethical instruction of their college as when in college they looked back to the admonitions of the nursery, and return to their alma mater in later years with much the feeling with which a man visits a kindly old grandmother.

But commencements certainly draw forth nothing so curious as the newspaper article addressed to the graduating class, and which now seems to be a regular part of the summer's editorial work. It seems to have one object in view, and only one, and that is preventing the graduate from thinking much of his education and his degree, or supposing that they will be of any particular use to him in his entrance on life, or make him any more acceptable to the community. He is warned that they will raise him in nobody's estimation, and prove rather a hinderance than a help to him in getting a living, and that it will be well for him to begin his career by trying to forget that he has ever been in college at all. Not unfrequently the discourse closes with a suggestion or hint that the best university is, after all, the office of "a great daily," and that the kindest thing a fond father could do for a promising boy would be to start him as a local reporter and make him get his first experience of life in the collection of "city items." There is in all this the expression, though in a somewhat grotesque form, of a widespread popular feeling that nothing is worthy of the name of education which does not fit a man to earn his bread rapidly and dexterously. Considering with how large a proportion of the human race the mere feeding and clothing of the body is the first and hardest of tasks, there is nothing at all surprising in this view. But the preservation and growth of civilization in any country depends much on the extent to which it is able out of its surplus production to provide some at least of its people with the means of cherishing and satisfying nobler appetites than hunger and thirst. The immense sum which is now spent every year on colleges--misspent though much of it may be--and the increasing number of students who throng to them, regardless of the fact that the training they get may make them at first feel a little strange and helpless in the fierce struggle for meat and drink, show that the increasing wealth of the nation is accompanied by an increasing recognition of the fact that life, after all, is not all living, that there are gains which cannot be entered in any ledger, and that a man may carry about with him, through a long and it may be outwardly unfortunate career, sources of pleasure and consolation which are none the less precious for being unsalable and invisible.

"ORGANS"

The untimely decease of the *Republic*, the paper which was set up some months ago to express in a semi-official way the views of the Administration and its immediate adherents on public questions, has a good deal that is tragic about it, as far as its principal conductor is concerned. That a man of as much experience of politics and of newspapers as Mr. Norvell, the editor, had, should have supposed it possible to start a daily morning paper in this city at a time when a successful daily is worth millions, and when there are four already in possession of the field, without any other claims on popular attention than its being the mouth-piece of the leading politicians of the party in power, and with a capital which in his dreams only reached $500,000, and in fact only $40,000, is a curious though sad illustration of the power of the press over the imagination even of persons long familiar with it. The failure of the enterprise, however distressing in some of its aspects, is valuable as establishing more conspicuously and firmly than ever two facts of considerable importance in relation to journalism. One is, that when politicians so deeply desire an organ as to be willing to set one up for the exclusive use of the party, it is a sure sign that the party is in serious danger of extinction. The other is, that the public mind is so fully made up that the position of a newspaper ought to be a judicial one, that all attempts to make a paper avowedly partisan can only be saved from commercial failure by large capital, extraordinary ability, and well-established prestige.

"Organs" took their rise when the sole use of a newspaper was to communicate intelligence, and when men in power found it convenient to have a channel through which they could let out certain things which they wished to be spread abroad. Out of this kind of relation to the Government a small paper, which did not object to the humble *role* of a sort of official gazette, from which the earlier newspapers indeed differed but little, could, of course, always get a livelihood, and perhaps a little of the dignity which comes from having or being supposed to have state secrets to keep. But the gradual addition to the "news-letter" of the sermon known as a "leader" or "editorial article" made the relation more and more difficult and finally impossible. The more pompous, portentous, and prophetic in their character the editor's comments on public affairs became, the less disposed was the public to allow him to retain the position of a paid agent of the State. It began to feel toward him as it would have felt toward the town-crier if he had put on a gown and bands, and insisted on accompanying his announcement of thefts and losses with homilies on the vanity of life and the right use of opportunities. The editor had, in short, to conduct his business in a manner befitting his newly assumed duties as a prophet, and to pretend at least that his utterances were wholly independent and were due simply to a desire for the public good, as a prophet's ought to be. It is now very rare indeed that a government is able to induce a well-established newspaper of the first class to act as its organ in the proper sense of that term, except by working on the vanity of editors. Almost all editors are a little sensitive about the imputation of being mere commentators or critics, and a little desirous of being thought "practical men," by those engaged in the actual working of political machinery. The "old editor" in this country in fact preferred to be thought a working politician, and liked to use his paper as a piece of political machinery for producing solid party gains, and in this way to be received into the circle of "workers" and "managers" as one of themselves; and to retain this position he was always willing to "write up" any view they suggested. His successor, though he cares less about being "a worker," and is able to secure the attendance of politicians at his office without running after them, is, nevertheless, more or less flattered by the confidences of men in power, and it often takes only a small amount of these confidences to make him surrender the judicial position and accept that of an advocate, and stand by them through thick and thin. But no leading journal has ever tried this position in our day very long without being forced out of it by the demand of the public for impartiality and the consequent difficulty of avoiding giving offence in official quarters. Every administration does things either through its chief or subordinates which will not bear defence, and which its judicious friends prefer to pass over in silence. But a journalist cannot keep silent. The Government may require him to hold his tongue, but the reader demands that he shall speak; and as the public supplies the sinews of war, and pays for the prophet's robes, he is sooner or later compelled to break with the Government and to reproach it for not listening to the advice of its friends in time.

Moreover, in a country in which the press is free and newspapers abound, a party which contains a majority of the people cannot fail to have the support of a large and influential portion of the press. Its conductors, though prophets, do not wear camel's hair, nor is their diet locusts and wild honey. They form part of the community, live among the voters, and share, to a greater or less extent, their prejudices and expectations and sympathies. Every party, therefore, is sure, as long as it has a strong hold on the public, of having a strong hold on the press, and of having a considerable number of the most influential editors among its defenders. One of the sure signs that it is losing its hold on the public is the defection of the press or its growing lukewarmness. Newspapers cannot, perhaps, build a party up or pull one down, but when you see the newspapers deserting a party it is all but proof that the agencies which dissolve a political organization are at work. The successful editors may have no originating power or no organizing power, and no capacity for legislation, and may even want the prophetic instinct; but a certain intuitive sense of the direction in which the tide of popular feeling is running is the principal condition of their success, and an anxious politician may therefore always safely credit them with possessing it. If they had not had it, their papers would not have succeeded.

If the incident or its lessons should result in establishing better relations between political men and the press, the sacrifice of the unfortunate projector of the *Republic* will, however, be a small price to pay for a great gain. We do not, as our readers know, set up to be champions of the press, and have certainly never shown any disposition to underrate its defects or shortcomings. But there is one thing which no candid and careful observer can avoid seeing, and that is that the press of the country, as an instrument of discussion and popular education, has undergone within twenty years an improvement nothing analogous to which is to be found in the class of politicians. The newspapers are now, in the vast majority of cases in all our leading cities, conducted by men who are familiar with the leading ideas of our time and with the latest advances in science and the art, including the art of government, and who write under the influence of these ideas and these advances, and who have consequently got a standard of efficiency in legislative administration which has not yet made its way into the political class. The result is that, after making all possible allowance for the carelessness and recklessness and dishonesty of reporters, and the personal biases and enmities of editors, the men who carry on the Government, excepting a few experts, have become objects of criticism on the part of the daily press, the depreciatory tone of which is not wholly unjustifiable or unnatural, and politicians repay this contempt with a hatred which is none the less fierce for having no adequate means of expression.

EVIDENCE ABOUT CHARACTER

There has been during the week a loud and increasing demand for the application of the legal process of discovering truth to the Tilton-Beecher case. People ask that it be carried into court, not only because all witnesses might thus be compelled to appear and testify, but because apparently there is, in the minds of many, a peculiar virtue in "the rules of evidence" used by lawyers. Witnesses examined under these rules are supposed to receive from them a strong stimulus in veracity and explicitness, while they at once expose prevarication or concealment. One newspaper eulogist went so far the other day as to pronounce the rules the product of the wisdom of all ages, beginning with the Phoenicians and coming down to our own time. There is, however, only one good reason that we know of for carrying any attack on character into court, and that is the obvious one, that the courts only can compel those who are supposed to know anything about a matter of litigation to appear and state it. But we do not know of any other advantage which can be claimed for a trial in court, in such a case, over a trial before a well-selected lay tribunal. "The rules of evidence" in use in our courts are not, as too many persons seem to suppose, deductions from the constitution of the human mind, or, in other words, natural rules for the discovery of truth under all conditions. On the contrary, they are a system of artificial presumptions created for the use of a tribunal of a somewhat low order of intelligence, and are intended to produce certain well-defined and limited results, which the law considers generally beneficial. They have, that is to say, grown up for the use of the jury. The large number of exclusions which they contain are due simply to a desire to prevent jurymen's being confused by kinds of testimony which they are not supposed to have learning or acumen enough to weigh. If anyone will go into the City Hall and listen to the trial of even a trifling cause, he will find that the proceedings consist largely in the attempt of one lawyer to have certain facts laid before the jury and the attempts of the other to prevent it, the judge sitting as arbiter between them and applying the rules of admission and exclusion to each of these facts as it comes up. If he examines, too, in each instance what it is that is thus pertinaciously offered and pertinaciously opposed, he will find that it almost invariably has *something* to do with the controversy before the court--it may be near or more remote--but still something. Consequently it has, logically, a certain bearing on the case, or is, under the constitution of the human mind, proper evidence. When the judge says it is irrelevant, he does not mean that it is logically irrelevant; he means that it has been declared irrelevant on certain grounds of expediency by the system of jurisprudence which he administers. He refuses to let it go to the jury because he thinks it would befog them or turn their attention away from the "legal issue" or, in other words, from the one little point on which the law compels the plaintiff and defendant to concentrate their dispute, in order to render it triable at all by the peculiar tribunal which the Anglo-Saxon race has chosen for the protection of its rights.

It follows that our rules of evidence are unknown on the European continent and in every country in which courts are composed of judges only--that is, of men with special training and capacity for the work of weighing testimony--or in which the legal customs have been created by such courts. There the litigants follow the natural order, and carry with them before the bench everything that has any relation to the case whatever, and leave the court to examine it and allow it its proper force. Our own changes in the law of evidence are all in this direction. The amount of excluded testimony--that is, of testimony with which we are afraid to trust the jury--has been greatly diminished during the last few years, and, considering the growth of popular intelligence, properly diminished. The tendency of legislation now is toward letting the jury hear everybody--the plaintiff and defendant, the prisoner, the wife, the husband, and the witness with a pecuniary interest in the result of the trial--and put its own estimate on what the testimony amounts to. But nevertheless, even now, who is there that has ever watched the preparation of a cause for trial who has not listened to lamentations over the difficulty or impossibility of getting this or that important fact before the jury, or has not witnessed elaborate precautions, on one side or another, to prevent some fact from getting before the jury? The skill of a counsel in examining or cross-examining a witness, for instance, is shown almost as much by what he avoids bringing out as by what he brings out, and no witness is allowed to volunteer any statement lest he should tell something which, however pertinent in reality, the rules pronounce inadmissible.

Now, rules of this kind are singularly unsuited to the conduct of inquiries touching character. It is true the law provides a process nominally for the vindication of character, called an action for libel, but the remedy it supplies is not a vindication properly so called, but a sum of money as a kind of penalty on the libeller, not for having assailed you, but for not having been able to prove his case under the rules of evidence. In a suit for libel, too, the parties fight their battle in the strict legal order--the plaintiff, that is to say, stands by and challenges the defendant to produce his proofs, and then fights bitterly through his counsel to keep out as much of the proof as he can. He supplies no evidence himself that is not strictly called for, and proffers no explanation that does not seem necessary to procure an award of pecuniary damages, and takes all the pains possible to bring confusing influences to bear on the jury. When we consider, too, that the jury is composed of men who may be said to be literally called in from the street, without the slightest regard to their special qualifications for the conduct of any inquiry, and that they are apt to represent popular passions and prejudices in all conspicuous and exciting cases, we easily see why a trial by a jury, under the common-law rules of evidence, is not the process through which a high-minded man who sought not for "damages," but to keep his reputation absolutely spotless in the estimation of his neighbors, would naturally seek his vindication.

It cannot be too often said, in these times when great reputations are so often assailed and so often perish, that nobody who has not deliberately chosen the life of a stoical recluse is justified either in refusing to defend his reputation or in defending it by technical processes if any others are within his reach. It is, of course, open to any man to say that he cares nothing for the opinion of mankind, and will not take the trouble to influence it in any manner in regard to himself. But, if he says so, he is bound not to identify with himself, in any manner, either great interests or great causes. If he makes himself the champion of other people's rights, or the exponent of important principles, or has through any power of his achieved an influence over other people's minds sufficiently great to make it appear that certain doctrines or ideas must stand or fall by him, he has surrendered his freedom in all that regards the maintenance of his fame.

It is no longer his only to maintain. It has become, as it were, embodied in popular morality, been made the basis of popular hopes, and a test under which popular faith or approval is bestowed on a great variety of ways and means of living. Such a man is bound to defend himself from the instant at which he finds the assaults on him begin to tell on the public conception of his character. Dignified reserve is a luxury in which it is not permitted to him to indulge; and when he comes to defend himself, it must not be with the calculating shrewdness of the strategist or tactician. The only rules of evidence of which he can claim the benefit are the laws of the human mind. The tribunal, too, before which he seeks reparation should not be what the state supplies only, but the very best he can reach, and it should, if possible, be composed of men with no motive for saving him and with no reason for hating him, and with such training and experience as may best fit them for the task of weighing his enemy's charges and his own excuses and explanations. His course before such a tribunal, too, should be marked by ardor rather than by prudence. He should chafe under delay, clamor for investigation, and invite scrutiny, and put away from him all advisers whose experience is likely to incline them to chicane or make them satisfied with a technical victory. Such men are always dangerous in delicate cases. He should not wait for his accuser to get in all his case if the substantial part of it is already before the court, because his answer ought not, as in a court of law, to cover the complaint simply and no more. It ought to contain a plain unvarnished tale of the whole transaction, and not those parts only which the accusation may have touched, because his object is not only to wrest a verdict of "not proven" from his judges, but to satisfy even the timid and sensitive souls whose faith in their idols is so large a part of their moral life, not only that he is not guilty, but that he never even inclined toward guilt.

PHYSICAL FORCE IN POLITICS

The late discussion on the possibility or expediency of maintaining governments at the South which had no physical force at their disposal has not failed to attract the attention of the friends of woman suffrage. They see readily what, indeed, most outsiders have seen all along, that the failure of the numerical majority in certain Southern States to hold the power to which the law entitled them simply because they were unable or unwilling to fight, has a very important bearing on the fitness of women to participate in the practical work of government, and a well-known writer, "T. W. H.," in a late number of the ***Woman's Journal***, endeavors to show that what has happened at the South is full of encouragement for the woman suffragists. His argument is in substance this: You (the opponents) have always maintained as the great objection to the admission of women to the franchise, that if women voted, cases might arise in which the physical force of the community would be in the hands of one party and the legal authority in those of the other, and we should then witness the great scandal of a majority government unable to execute the laws. We have just seen at the South, however, that the possession of physical force is not always sufficient to put the majority even of the male voters in possession of the Government. In South Carolina and Louisiana the Government has been seized and successfully held by a minority, in virtue of their greater intelligence and self-confidence. To use his own language:

"The present result in South Carolina is not a triumph of bodily strength over weakness, but, on the contrary, of brains over bodily strength. And however this reasoning affects the condition of South Carolina--which is not here my immediate question--it certainly affects, in a very important degree, the argument for woman suffrage. If the ultimate source of political power is muscle, as is often maintained, then woman suffrage is illogical; but if the ultimate source of political power is, as the Nation implies, 'the intelligence, sagacity, and the social and political experience of the population,' then the claims of women are not impaired. For we rest our case on the ground that women equal men on these points, except in regard to political experience, which is a thing only to be acquired by practice.

"So the showing of the ***Nation*** is, on the whole, favorable to women. It looks in the direction of Mr. Bagehot's theory, that brains now outweigh muscle in government. Just in proportion as man becomes civilized and comes to recognize laws as habitually binding, does the power of mere brute force weaken. In a savage state the ruler of a people must be physically as well as mentally the strongest; in a civilized state the commander-in-chief may be physically the weakest person in the army. The English military power is no less powerful for obeying the orders of a queen. The experience of South Carolina does not vindicate, but refutes, the theory that muscle is the ruling power. It shows that an educated minority is more than a match for an ignorant majority, even though this be physically stronger. Whether this forbodes good or evil to South Carolina is not now the question; but so far as woman suffrage is concerned, the moral is rather in its favor than against it."

What is singular in all this is, that the writer is evidently under the impression that the term "physical force" in politics means muscle, or, to put the matter plainly, that the fact that the South Carolina negroes, who unquestionably surpass the whites in lifting power, could not hold their own against them, shows that government has become a mere question of brains, and that as women have plenty of brains, though they can lift very little, they could perfectly well carry on, or help to carry on, a government which has only moral force on its side.

Now, as a matter of fact, there has been no recent change in the meaning attached to "physical force" in political nomenclature. It does not mean muscle or weight now, as we see in South Carolina; and it has never meant muscle or weight since the dawn of civilization. The races and nations which have made civilization and ruled the world have done so by virtue of their possessing the very superiority, in a greater or less degree, which the Carolina whites have shown in their late struggle with the blacks. The Greeks, the Romans, the Turks, the English, the French, and the Germans have all succeeded in government--that is, in seizing and keeping power--not through superiority of physical force which consists in muscle, but through the superiority which consists in the ability to organize and bring into the field, and reinforce large bodies of men, with the resolution to kill and be killed in order to have their own way in disputes. No matter how much intelligence a people may have, unless they are able and willing to apply their intelligence to the art of war, and have the personal courage necessary to carry out in action the plans of their leaders, they cannot succeed in politics. Brains are necessary for political success, without doubt, but it must be brains applied, among other things to the organization of physical force in fleets and armies. An "educated minority," as such, is no more a match for a "physically stronger ignorant majority" than a delicate minister for a pugilist in "condition," unless it can furnish well-equipped and well-led troops. The Greeks were better educated than the Romans, but this did not help them. The Romans of the Empire were vastly more intelligent and thoughtful than the Barbarians, but they could not save the Empire. The Italians of the Middle Ages were the superiors of the French and Germans in every branch of culture, and yet this did not prevent Italy being made the shuttlecock of northern politicians and free-booters. The French overran Germany in the beginning of the present century, and the Germans have overrun France within the last ten years, not in either case owing to superiority in lifting or boxing, or in literary "culture," but to superiority in the art of fighting-- that is, of bringing together large bodies of armed men who will not flinch, and will advance when ordered on the battle-field.

It is skill in this art which is meant by the term "physical force" in politics, and it is this physical force which lies behind all successful government. The superiority of the North in numbers, wealth, machinery, literature, and common schools would have profited it nothing, and the American Republic would have disappeared from the map if it had not been possible, thirty years ago, to apply a vast amount of intelligence to the purposes of destruction, and to find large numbers of men willing to fight under orders. In quiet times, under a government in which the numerical majority and the intelligence and property of the community are on the same side, and take substantially the same views of public polity, and the display of coercive force, except for ordinary police purposes, is not called for, we not unnaturally slide readily into the pleasant belief that government is purely a moral agency, and that people obey the law through admiration of intellectual power and the dread of being "cornered" in argument, or of being exposed as selfish or lawless.

Such occurrences as the late civil war and the recent deadlock at the South are very useful in uncovering the secret springs of society, and reminding people of the tremendous uncertainties and responsibilities by which national as well as individual life is surrounded, reminding the voter, in short, that he may not always be able to discharge his duty to the country by depositing his ballot in the box; that he may have to make the result sure by putting everything he values in the world at stake. The poor negroes in South Carolina have not been deposed simply because they are ignorant; the Russian peasants who fought at Borodino were grossly ignorant. How many of the English hinds who stood rooted in the soil at Waterloo could read and write? The Carolinian majority failed because it did not contain men willing to fight, or leaders capable of organization for military purposes, or, in other words, did not possess what has since the dawn of civilization been the first and greatest title to political power. The Carolinian minority did not drive their opponents out of the offices by simply offering the spectacle of superior intelligence of self-confidence, but by the creation of a moral certainty that, if driven to extremities, they would outdo the Republicans in the marshalling, marching, provisioning, and manoeuvring of riflemen.

If this be true, it will be readily seen that the lesson of the South Carolina troubles, far from containing encouragement for the friends of female suffrage, is full of doubt and difficulty. Those who believe that women voters would constitute a new and valuable force in politics must recognize the possibility that they would at some time or other constitute the bulk of a majority claiming the government, and they must also recognize the probability that the male portion of this majority would be composed of the milder and less energetic class of men, people with much brains and but little physical courage, ready to go to the stake for a conviction, but not ready to shoulder a musket or assault a redoubt. If under these circumstances the minority, composed exclusively of men, inferior if you will, to the majority in the purity of their motives, the breadth of their culture, and in capacity for drawing constitutions and laws and administering charities, should refuse to obey the majority, and should say that its government was a ridiculous "fancy" government, administered by crackbrained people, and likely to endanger property and the public credit, and that it must be abolished, what would the women and their "gentlemen friends" do? They would doubtless remonstrate with the recusants and show them the wickedness of their course, but then the recusants would be no more moved by this than Wade Hampton and his people by Mr. Chamberlain's eloquent and affecting inaugural address. They would tell the ladies that their intelligence was doubtless of a high order, and their aims noble, but that as they were apparently unable to supply policemen to arrest the persons who disobeyed their laws, their administration was a farce and its disappearance called for in the interest of public safety. Accordingly it would be removed to the great garret of history, to lie side by side with innumerable other disused plans for human improvement.

The cause of much of the misconception about the part played by physical force in modern society now current in reformatory circles is doubtless to be found in the disappearance of sporadic and lawless displays of it, such as, down to a very recent period, seriously disturbed even the most civilized communities. The change that has taken place, however, consists not in the total disuse of force as a social agency, but in the absorption of all force by the government, making it so plainly irresistible that the occasions are rare when anything approaching to organized resistance or defiance of it is attempted. When it lays its commands on a man he knows that obedience will, if necessary, be enforced by an agency of such tremendous power that he does not think of revolt. But it is not the high intelligence of those who carry it on that he bows to; it is to their ability to crush him like an egg-shell. Of course, it is not surprising that his submissiveness should at meetings of philanthropists be ascribed to the establishment of a consensus between his mind and the mind of the law-giver, or in other words, the subjection of society to purely moral influences; but it is perhaps well that complications like those of South Carolina should now and then occur to infuse sobriety into speculation and explain the machinery of civilization.

"COURT CIRCLES"

The passionate excitement created in Canada by the arrival of a daughter of the Queen, and the prospect of the establishment of "a court" in Ottawa which will have the appearance of a real Court--that is, a court with blood royal in it, instead of a court held merely by the queen's legal representatives--is a phenomenon of considerable interest. It affords a fresh illustration of that growth of reverence for royalty which all the best observers agree has for the last forty years been going on in England, side by side with the growth of democratic feeling and opinion in politics--that is, the sovereign has more than gained as a social personage what she has lost as a political personage. The less she has had to do with the government the more her drawing-rooms have been crowded, and the more eager have people become for personal marks of her favor.

The reason of this is not far to seek. It lies in the enormous increase during that period in the size of the class which is not engaged in that, to the heralds, accursed thing--trade, and has money enough to bear the expense of "a presentation," and of living or trying to live afterward in the circle of those who might be invited to court, or might meet the Prince of Wales at dinner. The accumulation of fortunes since the Queen's accession has been very great, and they have, however made, come into possession now of a generation which has never been engaged in any occupation frowned on by the Lord Chamberlain, and which owns estates, or at all events possesses all outward marks of gentility, when it has been received by the Queen, and has got into Burke's Dictionary at the end of an interesting though perhaps apocryphal genealogy. This reception is the crown of life's struggle, a sort of certificate that the hero or heroine of it is fit company for anybody in the world. It is, in fact, a social graduation. When you get somebody who is himself a graduate to agree to present you, and the Lord Chamberlain, after examining your card, makes no objection to you, he virtually furnishes you with a sort of diploma which guarantees you against what may be called authorized snubs. People may afterward decline your invitations on the ground that they do not like you, or that your entertainments bore them, but not on the ground that your social position is inferior to their own.

That the struggle for this diploma in a wealthy and large society should be great and increasing is nothing wonderful. The desire for it among the women especially, to whose charge the creation and preservation of "position" are mainly committed, is very deep. It inflames their imagination in a way which makes husbands ready for anything in order to get it, and in fact makes it indispensable to their peace of mind and body that they should get it as soon as their pecuniary fortune seems to put it within their reach. Since the Queen ascended the throne the population has risen from 20,000,000 to 35,000,000, and the number of great fortunes and presentable people has increased in a still greater ratio, and the pressure on the court has grown correspondingly; but there remains after all only one court to gratify the swarm of new applicants. The colonies, too, have of late years contributed largely to swell the tide. Every year London society and the ranks of the landed gentry are reinforced by returned Australians and New Zealanders and Cape-of-Good-Hopers and China and India merchants, who feel that their hard labors and long exile have left life empty and joyless until they see the names of their wives and daughters in the *Gazette* among the presentations at a drawing-room or levee.

In the colonies, and especially in Canada, where there is so little in the local life to gratify the imagination, the court shines with a splendor which the distance only intensifies. To a certain class of Canadians, who enjoy more frequent opportunities than the inhabitants of the other great colonies of renewing or fortifying their love of the competition of English social life, and of the marks of success in it, the court, as the fountain of honor, apart from all political significance, is an object of almost fierce interest. In England itself the signs of social distinction are not so much prized. This kind of Canadian is, in fact, apt to be rather more of an Englishman than the Englishman himself in all these things. He imitates and cultivates English usages with a passion which takes no account of the restrictions of time or place. It is "the thing" too in Canadian society, as in the American colony in Paris, to be much disgusted by the "low Americans" who invade the Dominion in summer, and to feel that even the swells of New York and Boston could achieve much improvement in their manners by faithful observation of the doings in the Toronto and Ottawa drawing-rooms.

As far as admiration of courts and a deep desire for court-life and a belief in the saving grace of contact with royalty can go, therefore, there are Canadians fully prepared for the establishment of a court "in their midst." The society of the province was, in fact, in an imflammable eagerness to kiss hands, and back out from the presence of royalty, and perform the various exercises pertaining to admission to court circles, and in a proper state of Jingo distrust of the wicked Czar and his minions--which in the Colonies is now one of the marks of gentility--when the magician, Lord Beaconsfield, determined to apply the match to it by sending out a real princess. In spite of his contempt for the "flat-nosed Franks," however, he can hardly have been prepared for the response which he elicited. He cannot have designed to make monarchy and royalty seem ridiculous, and yet the articles and addresses and ceremonies with which the new Governor-General and his wife have been received look as if the Minister had determined, before he died, to have the best laugh of his farcical career over the barbarians who have called him in to rule over them. A court is a very delicate thing, and a strong capacity for enjoying it does not of itself make good courtiers. In England the reasons which prevent a man's being received at court--such as active prosecution of the dry-goods business--are a thousand years old; in fact, they may be said to have come down from the ancient world along with the Roman law. They have, therefore, a certain natural fitness and force in the eyes of the natives of that country. That is, it seems to "stand to reason" that a trader should not go to court. Moreover, they can be enforced in England and still leave an abundant supply of spotless persons for the purposes of court society. The court-line is drawn along an existing and well-marked social division.

In Canada this preparation for court gayeties does not exist. If the persons soiled by commerce were to be excluded from the princess's presence, she would lead a lonely and dismal life, and the court would be substantially a failure. If, on the other hand, the court is to be made up exclusively of rich traders, it will not only excite the fiercest jealousies and bitterness among those who are excluded, but it will be very difficult to provide a rule for passing on claims for presentation when once the line of official position is passed. But, it may be said, why not throw all restrictions aside and admit everybody, as at White House receptions? Nobody will ask this question who has mastered even the rudiments of royalty, and we shall not take the trouble of answering it fully. We are now discussing the question for the benefit of persons of some degree of knowledge. Suffice it to say that any laxity of practice at Ottawa would do a good deal of damage to the monarchical principle itself, which, as Mr. Bagehot has pointed out, owes much of its force and permanence even in England to its hold on the imagination. The princess cannot go back to England receiving Tom, Dick, and Harry in Canada without a certain loss of prestige both for herself and her house.

Not the least curious feature of the crisis is the interest the prospect of a Canadian court has excited in this country. Our newspapers know what they are about when they give whole pages to accounts of the voyage and the reception, including a history of the House of Argyll and a brief sketch of the feelings of Captain the Duke of Edinburgh, now on the Halifax Station, over his approaching meeting with his sister. They recognize the existence of a deep and abiding curiosity, at least among the women of our country, about all that relates to royalty and its doings, in spite of the labor expended for nearly a century by orators and editors in showing up the vanity and hollowness of monarchical distinctions. In fact, if the secrets of American hearts could be revealed, we fear it would be found that the materials for about a million of each order of nobility, from dukes down, exist among us under quiet republican exteriors, and that if a court circle were set up among us no earthly power could prevent its assuming unnatural and unmanageable proportions. A prince like the late Emperor Maximilian, whose purse was meagre but whose connection with a reigning house was unquestioned and close, might find worse ways of repairing his fortune than setting up an amateur court in some of the Atlantic cities and charging a moderate fee for presentation, and drawing the line judiciously so as to keep up the distinction without damaging his revenues. To prevent cutting remarks on the members of the circle, however, and too much ridicule of the whole enterprise, he would have to give the editors high places about his person, and provide offices for the reporters in his basement. If the scheme were well organized and did not attempt too much, its value in settling people's "position," and in giving the worthy their proper place without the prolonged struggles they now have sometimes to undergo, would be very great, and it would enable foreign students of our institutions to pursue successfully certain lines of inquiry into our manners and customs in which they are now too often baffled.

LIVING IN EUROPE AND GOING TO IT

Every year a great deal of discussion of the best mode of spending the summer, and the course of the people who go to Europe, instead of submitting to the discomfort and extortion of American hotels, is for the most part greatly commended. The story told about the hotels and lodging-houses is the same every year. The food is bad, the rooms uncomfortable, and the charges high. The fashion, except perhaps at Newport and Beverly, near Boston, Bar Harbor, and one or two other highly favored localities, grows stronger and stronger, to live in the city in the winter and spend the three hot months in France or England or Switzerland. Moreover, the accounts which come from Europe of the increase in the number of American colonists now to be found in every attractive town of the Continent are not exactly alarming, but they are sufficient to set people thinking. The number of those who pass long years in Europe, educate their children there, and retain little connection with America beyond drawing their dividends, grows steadily, and as a general rule they are persons whose minds or manners or influence makes their prolonged absence a sensible loss to our civilization. Moreover, when they come back, they find it difficult to stay, and staying is not made easy for them. People here are a little suspicious of them, and are apt to fancy that they have got out of sympathy with American institutions, and have grown too critical for the rough processes by which the work of life in America has in a large degree to be done. They themselves, on the other hand, besides being soured by the coldness of their reception, are apt to be disgusted by the want of finish of all their surroundings, by the difficulty with which the commoner and coarser needs are met in this country, and by the reluctance with which allowance is made by legislation and opinion for the gratification of unusual or unpopular tastes.

The result is a breach, which is already wide, and tends to widen, between the class which is hard at work making its fortune and the class which has either made its fortune or has got all it desires, which is the same thing as a fortune. There is a great deal of work which this latter would like to do. There is a great deal of the work of legislation and administration and education for which it is eminently fitted, but in which, nevertheless, it has little or no chance of sharing, owing to the loss of the art of winning the confidence of others, and working with others, which is more easily learned in America than elsewhere, and which is readily lost by prolonged residence in any European country, and the absence of which here makes all other gifts for practical purposes almost worthless. So that it must be said that the amount of intellectual and aesthetic culture which an American acquires in Europe is somewhat dearly purchased. When he gets home, he is apt to find it a useless possession, as far as the world without is concerned, unless he is lucky enough, as sometimes but not often happens, to drop into some absorbing occupation or to lose his fortune. Failing this, he begins that melancholy process of vibration between the two continents in which an increasingly large number of persons pass a great part of their lives, their hearts and affections being wholly in neither.

The remedy for the mania for *living* abroad is an elaborate one, and one needing more time for its creation. No country retains the hearty affection of its educated class which does not feed its imagination. The more we cultivate men, the higher their ideals grow in all directions, political and social, and they like best the places in which these ideals are most satisfied. The long and varied history of older countries offers their citizens a series of pictures which stimulate patriotism in the highest degree; and it will generally be found that the patriotism and love of home of the cultivated class is in the ratio of the supply of this kind of food. They are languid among the Russians, and among the Germans prior to the late war, as compared to the English and French. In default of a long history, however, historic incidents are apt to lose their power on the imagination through over-use. The jocose view of Washington and of the Pilgrim Fathers, of Bunker Hill and of the Fourth of July, already gains ground rapidly among us, through too great familiarity. When Professor Tyndall, in one of his lectures here, made an allusion which he meant to be solemn and impressive, to Plymouth Rock, its triteness drew a titter from the audience which for a moment confounded him.

Unluckily, history cannot be made to order. It is the product of ages. The proper substitute for it, as well as for the spectacular effects of monarchy, in new democratic societies, is perfection. There is no way in which we can here kindle the imaginations of the large body of men and women to whom we are every year giving an increasingly high education so well as by finish in the things we undertake to do. Nothing does so much to produce despondency about the republic, or alienation from republican institutions, among the young of the present day, as the condition of the civil service, the poor working of the post-office and the treasury or the courts, or the helplessness of legislators in dealing with the ordinary everyday problems. The largeness of the country, and the rapidity of its growth, and the comparatively low condition of foreign nations in respect to freedom, which roused people in Fourth-of-July orations forty years ago, have, like the historical reminiscences, lost their magic, and the material prosperity is now associated in people's minds with so much moral corruption that the mention of it produces in some of the best of us a feeling not far removed from nausea. Nothing will do so much now to rouse the old enthusiasm as the spectacle of the pure working of our administrative machinery, of able and independent judges, a learned and upright bar, a respectable and purified custom-house, an enlightened and efficient treasury, and a painstaking post-office. The colleges of the country and the railroads, and indeed everything that depends on private enterprise, are rapidly becoming objects of pride; but a good deal needs to be done by the government to prevent its being a source of shame.

Mrs. Stevenson, a Philadelphia lady; the president of the Civic Club in that city, delivered an address to the club some weeks ago on its work of reform, in which we find the following passage:

"There seems to exist a mysterious, unwritten law governing the social organism which causes a natural and wholesome reaction to take place whenever tendencies, perhaps inherent in certain classes, threaten to become general, and thereby dangerous to the community. A few years ago, for instance, with the increasing facilities for foreign travel, and the corresponding increase of international intercourse, Anglomania had become so much in vogue as to form an incipient danger to the true democratic American spirit that constitutes the real strength of our nation. It was fast becoming a national habit to extol everything European--from monarchy and its aristocratic institutions down to the humblest article of dress or of household use--to the detriment of everything American; and from the upper 'four hundred' this habit was fast extending to the upper forty thousand. But just as our wealthy classes were beginning to make themselves positively ridiculous abroad, and almost intolerable at home, a reaction set in, and upon all sides there sprang up patriotic associations of a social order--'Sons and Daughters of the Revolution,' 'Colonial Dames,' etc.--which revived proper American self-respect among our people by teaching us to rest our pride, if pride we *must* have, where it legitimately should rest--upon good service rendered to our own country."

This seems to be a shaft aimed at the practice of "going to Europe," for the decline of "the true American spirit" and the growth of Anglomania are ascribed to the "increasing facilities for foreign travel" and "the corresponding increase of international intercourse." If the charge be true, it is one of the most afflicting over made, because it shows that "the true democratic American spirit" suffers from what the world has hitherto considered one of the greatest triumphs of modern science, and one of the greatest blessings conferred on the race--the enormous improvement in oceanic steam navigation; that, in fact, American patriotism is very much like the Catholic faith in the Middle Ages--something naturally hostile to progress in the arts.

If, too, the practice of going to Europe be dangerous to American faith and morals, the number of those who go makes it of immense importance. There is probably no American who has risen above very narrow circumstances who does not go to Europe at least once in his life. There is hardly a village in the country in which the man who has succeeded in trade or commerce does not announce his success to his neighbors by a trip to Europe for himself and his family. There is hardly a professor, or teacher, or clergyman, or artist, or author who does not save out of a salary, however small, in order to make the voyage. Tired professional or business men make it constantly, under the pretence that it is the only way they can get "a real holiday." Journalists make it as the only way of getting out of their heads such disgusting top- ics as Croker and Gilroy, and Hill and Murphy. Rich people make it every year, or oftener, through mere restlessness. We are now leaving out of account, of course, immigrants born in the Old World, who go back to see their friends. We are talking of native Americans. Of course, all native Americans cannot go, because, even when they can afford it, they cannot always get the time. But we venture on the proposi- tion that there is hardly any American "in this broad land," as members of Congress say, who, having both time and money, has not gone to Europe, or does not mean to go some day or other. So that, if Mrs. Stevenson's account of the moral effects of the voyage were true, it would show that the very best portion of our population, the most moral, the most religious, and the most educated were constantly exposing themselves by tens of thousands to most debasing influences.

But is it true? We think not. Americans who go to Europe with some knowl- edge of history, of the fine arts, and of literature, all recognize the fact that they could not have completed their education without going. To such people travel in Europe is one of the purest and most elevating of pleasures, for Europe contains the experience of mankind in nearly every field of human endeavor. They often, it is true, come back discontented with America, but out of this discontent have grown some of our most valuable improvements--libraries, museums, art-galleries, col- leges. What they have seen in Europe has opened their eyes to the possibilities and shortcomings of their own country.

To take a familiar example, it is travel in Europe which has done most to stimu- late the movement for municipal reform. It is seeing London and Paris, and Berlin and Birmingham, which has done most to wake people up to the horrors of the Croker-Gilroy rule, and inflame the determination to end it as a national disgrace. The class of Americans who do not come back discontented are usually those who had no education to start with.

> "Knowledge to their eyes her ample page,
>   Rich with the spoils of time, did ne'er unroll!"

So, even when standing on the Acropolis at Athens or in the Tribuna at Florence, they feel themselves sadly "out of it." They think longingly of Billy or Jimmy, and the coffee and cakes of their far Missouri or Arkansas home, and come back cursing Europe and its contents. No damage is ever done by foreign travel to the "true democratic American spirit" of this class.

And now as to "Anglomania," a subject to be handled with as much delicacy as an anarchist bomb. Anglomania in one form or other is to be met with in all countries, especially France and Germany, and has shown itself here and there all over the Continent ever since the peace of 1815. The things in which it most imitates the English are riding, driving, men's clothes, sports in general, and domestic comfort. The reason is that the English have for two centuries given more attention to these things than any other people. No other has so cultivated the horse for pleasure purposes. No other has devoted so much thought and money to suitability in dress and to field sports. No other has brought to such perfection the art of living in country houses. In all these things people who can afford it try to imitate them. We say, with a full consciousness of the responsibility which the avowal entails on us, that they do right. It is well in any art to watch and imitate the man who has best succeeded in it. The sluggard has been exhorted even to imitate the ant, and anyone who wishes to ride or drive well, or dress appropriately, or entertain in a country house, ought to study the way the English do these things, and follow their example, for anything worth doing ought to be done well. It is mostly in these things that Anglomania consists.

Mrs. Stevenson, we fear, exaggerates greatly the number of Anglomaniacs. A few dozen are as many as are to be found in any country, and any government or polity which their presence puts in peril ought to be overthrown, for assuredly it is rotten to the core. There is nothing, in fact, better calculated to make Americans hang their heads for shame than the list of small things which one hears from "good Americans," put our institutions in danger. We remember a good old publisher, in the days before international copyright, who thought we could not much longer stand the circulation of British novels. Their ideas, he said, were dangerous to a republic. An Anglomaniac can hardly turn up his trousers on Fifth Avenue without eliciting shrieks of alarm from the American patriot. And yet a more harmless creature really does not exist.

These matters are worth notice because we are the only great nation in the world whom people try to preach into patriotism. The natives of other countries love their country simply, naturally, and for the most part silently, as they love their mothers and their wives. But to get an American to do so he has, one would think, to be followed about by a preacher with a big stick exhorting him to be a "good American," or he will catch it. But nobody was ever preached into love of country. He may be preached into sacrifices in its behalf, but the springs of love cannot be got at by any system of persuasion. No man will love his country unless he feels it to be lovable; and it is to making it lovable that the exertions of those who have American patriotism in charge should be devoted.

Every Good American may take comfort in the fact that very few people indeed of any social or political value who have once lived in America ever want again to live in Europe, unless they go for purposes of study or education. For there is no question that there is no country in the world in which the atmosphere is so friendly, and in which one is so sure of sympathy in misfortune, of acceptance on his own merits independently of birth or money, and has so many opportunities of escape from the slings and arrows of outrageous fortune, as America. These are the things which, after all, in the vast majority of cases, win and hold the human heart; and a country which has them can well afford to let its citizens travel, and even let some of them "be early English if they can."

CARLYLE'S POLITICAL INFLUENCE

The numerous articles called forth by Carlyle's "Reminiscences," both in this country and in England, while varying greatly in the proportions in which they mix their praise and blame, leave no doubt that there has occurred a very strong revulsion of feeling about him, so strong in England that we are told that the subscriptions for a proposed memorial to him have almost if not entirely ceased. The censure which Carlyle's friends are visiting on Mr. Froude for his indiscretion in printing the book, though deserved, has done but little to mitigate the severity of the judgment passed on the writer himself. In fact, we are inclined to believe that Mr. Froude's want of judgment rather helps to deepen the surprise and disappointment with which the book has been received, as affording an additional proof of the feebleness of Carlyle's own powers in estimating the people about him. That, after heaping contempt on so many of whom the world has been accustomed to think highly, he should have retained to the last his confidence in, and respect for, a person capable of dealing his fame such a deadly blow as Mr. Froude, not unnaturally increases the irritation with which the public has read his recollections of his friends and contemporaries. The "disillusion and disenchantment" worked by the book, in so far as it affects Carlyle's fame as a prophet, is, of course, a misfortune, and a very serious one. What it was he preached when his preaching first startled the world, but very few now undertake to say, and these few by no means agree in their story. His influence, apparently, was not of the kind which reaches a man through articulate speech, but rather that which comes through the blast of a trumpet or the marching tune of a good band, and fills the heart with a feeling of capacity for high endeavor, though one cannot say in what particular field it is to be displayed. But though he founded no school and taught no system of morals, his eminence as a mere preacher was one of the very valuable possessions of the Anglo-Saxon world, as a sort of standing protest against the materialistic tendencies of the age; and this eminence rested a good deal on the popular conception of the elevation of his own character. This conception has undoubtedly, whether justly or unjustly, been greatly shaken, if not destroyed, by the revelation that invidious comparison between himself and others was almost a habit of his life; that, while preaching patient endurance, he did not himself endure patiently even the minor ills of existence; that, when looking at the fine equipages at Hyde Park Corner, he had to support himself by "sternly thinking"--"yes, and perhaps none of you could do what I am at;" that his mental attitude during the preparation of most of his books was that of a man not properly appreciated who was going to cast pearls before swine; or, in other words, the attitude of an ordinary literary man burdened with too much vanity for his powers, and more concerned about the effect his work was likely to have on his personal fortunes than on the mental or moral condition of the world. While full of contempt for sciolists and pretenders and newspapers, he wrote, and was ready to write, on the American war without any knowledge of the facts, and scorned Darwinism without ever bestowing a thought on it. Carlyle's public were long ago conscious, as one of his critics has said, that he canted prodigiously about cant, and talked voluminously in praise of silence; but then it recognized that much repetition has always the air of cant, and that to persuade men to be silent, as well as to do anything else, one must talk a great deal. A prophet has to be diffuse and loud, and often shrill, and his disciples will always forgive any number of mistakes in method or manner as long as they believe that behind the preaching there is perfect simplicity and self-forgetfulness. That this belief has been weakened in many minds with regard to Carlyle by the "Reminiscences" there is no question, and the consequence of it is that the Anglo Saxon world has lost one of its best possessions; and it is a kind of possession which no apologies or explanations, and no proof of Mr. Froude's indiscretion, can restore.

There is, however, some compensation in the catastrophe. If there was nothing positive in Carlyle's moral teachings, if nobody could extract from his earlier utterances anything more definite than advice to "be up and doing with a heart for every fate," there was in the political teachings of his later works something very positive and definite, and something which he managed to surround with some of the diviner light of his first arraignments of modern civilization. There is, for instance, nothing in literature more ingenious than the way in which he presents Cromwell as the apostle of "truth" during the campaigns in Ireland after the death of the King. He lets slip no opportunity of setting forth the importance of those military operations as a means of bringing "truth" to the Irish, so much so that the reader at last begins to expect the revelation of some formula in which the Lord-General presented the truth to them. But long before the end is reached one finds that the only truth which Cromwell was spreading in Ireland was the simple one that anybody who resisted him in arms would probably be knocked on the head. This collocation of truth and superiority of physical force, and of falsehood and weakness, was, in fact, worked into all Carlyle's writings of a political character, and did, through his writings, become a very positive political influence after the generation which was roused by the first blasts of his moral trumpet had grown old, or had passed away. To most men under fifty, in fact, Carlyle is more known as a very truculent political philosopher than as a moralist, and most of his later imitators--Mr. Froude for one--have imitated him rather in preparing the way of the Strong Man in government, and recommending the helpless and forlorn to strip for a salutary dozen on the bare back, than in preaching self-knowledge or the inner worship of the "veracities."

That the effect of this on English politics has been bad, and very bad, during the past thirty years few will deny. It beyond question has had an evil influence on English opinion both about Ireland and about India, and about the civil war in the United States. It had much to do with the production of that great scandal, the defence of Governor Eyre, by nearly the whole of London society. Nay, we think we are not far wrong in saying that it did much to prepare the way for that remarkable episode in English history, the late administration of Lord Beaconsfield, with its jingo fever; its lavish waste of blood and treasure; its ferocious assertion of the beauty of national selfishness; its contempt for all that portion of the population of Turkey which was weak and subject and unhappy. When one contrasts the spirit in which John Stuart Mill approached all such subjects in his day, his patient pursuit of the facts, his almost over-earnest efforts to get at the point of view of those who differed with him, his steady indifference to his own fame in dealing with all public questions, and then reads the contemptuous way in which Carlyle disposes of him in the "Reminiscences," one gets, we were going to say, an almost painful sense of the contrast between the influence of the two men on their day and generation.

In so far as the "Reminiscences," therefore, ruin Carlyle as a politician, their publication must be considered a gain for the English race. The particular political vice his influence fostered, that nobody who cannot thrash you in fight is worth listening to, is, it must be said, a vice peculiar to the English race. It is only in the Anglo-Saxon forum that a man of foreign birth and unfamiliar ways of thinking has to obtain a ***locus standi*** by making himself an object of physical terror. The story which has lately gone the rounds of the papers, of Carlyle's discussion with some Irishman who got the better of him in an argument in support of the logical right of the Irish to manage their own affairs, in which he met his opponent in the last resort in half-humorous vehemence by informing him that he would cut his throat before he would let him have his independence, is not a bad expression of the spirit which has governed English policy in dealing with dependent communities. There is a certain wisdom and justice in exacting from every malcontent who asks for great changes in his condition some strong proof of his earnestness; but it is a test which has to be applied with great discretion, which nations that have made a great fortune with a strong right hand are not likely to apply with discretion, and which is apt to make weakness seem ridiculous as well as contemptible. The history of English politics for fifty years at least has been the history of the efforts of the nation to accustom itself to some other than the English standard of political respectability, to familiarize itself with the idea that pacific people, and poor people, and queer people had something to say for themselves, and were entitled to a place in the world. To the success of that effort it is safe to say that Mr. Carlyle's political writings have been more or less of an obstacle, and that the destruction of his influence will contribute something to the solution of some of the more serious pending problems of English politics.

THE EVOLUTION OF THE SUMMER RESORT

Nothing is more remarkable in the history of American summering than the number of new resorts which are discovered and taken possession of by "the city people" every year, the rapid increase in the means of transportation both to the mountains and the sea, and the steady encroachments of the cottager on the boarder in all the more desirable resorts. The growth of the American watering-place, indeed, now seems to be as much regulated by law as the growth of asparagus or strawberries, and is almost as easy to foretell. The place is usually first discovered by artists in search of sketches, or by a family of small means in search of pure air, and milk fresh from the cow, and liberty--not to say license--in the matter of dress. Its development then begins by some neighboring farmer's agreeing to take them to board--a thing he has never done before, and does now unwillingly, and he is very uncertain what to charge for it. But at a venture he fixes what seems to him an enormous sum--say $5 to $7 a week for each adult. His ideas about food for city people are, however, very vague. The only thing about their tastes of which he feels certain is that what they seek in the country is, above all things, change, and that they accordingly do not desire what they get at home. Accordingly he furnishes them with a complete set of novelties in the matter of food and drink, forgetting, however, that they might have got them at home if they pleased. The tea and coffee and bread differ from what they are used to at home simply in being worse. He is, too, at the seaside, very apt to put them on an exclusively fish diet, in the belief that it is only people who live by the sea who get fish, and that city people, weary of meat, must be longing for fish. The boarders, this first summer, having persuaded him to take them, are of course too modest to remonstrate, or even to hint, and go on to the end eating what is set before them, and pretending to be thankful, and try to keep up their failing strength by being a great deal in the open air, and admiring the scenery. After they leave, he is apt to be astonished by the amount of cash he finds himself possessed of, probably more than he ever handled before at one time, except when he mortgaged his farm, and comes to the conclusion that taking summer boarders is an excellent thing, and worth cultivating.

In the next stage he seeks them, and perhaps is emboldened by the advice of somebody to advertise the place, and try to get hold of some editors or ministers whose names he can use as references, and who will talk it up. He soon secures one or two of each, and they then tell him that his house is frequented by intellectual or "cultured" people; and he becomes more elated and more enterprising, enlarges the dining-room, adds on a wing, relieves his wife of the cooking by hiring a woman in the nearest town, and gives more meat and stronger coffee, and, little by little, grows into a hotel-keeper, with an office and a register. His neighbors, startled by his success, follow his example, it may be only *longo intervallo*, and soon the place becomes a regular "resort," with girls and boys in white flannel, lawn-tennis (which succeeds croquet), a livery-stable, stages, an ice-cream store with a soda-water fountain, a new church, and with strange names taken out of books for the neighboring hills and lanes and brooks.

This stage may last for years--in some places it has been known to last thirty or forty without any change, beyond the opening of new hotels--and it becomes marked by crowds of people, who go back every year in the character of old boarders, get the best rooms, and are on familiar terms of friendship with the proprietor and the older waiter-girls.

But it may be brought to a close, and is now being brought to a close in scores of American watering-places, by the appearance of the cottager, who has become to the boarder what the red squirrel is to the gray, a ruthless invader and exterminator. The first cottager is almost always a boarder, so that there is no means of discovering his approach and resisting his advances. In nine cases out of ten he is a simple guest at the farm-house or the hotel, without any discoverable airs or pretensions, on whom the scenery has made such an impression that he quietly buys a lot with a fine view. The next year he builds a cottage on it, and gradually, and it may be at first imperceptibly, separates himself in feeling and in standards from his fellow-boarders. The year after he is in the cottage, and the mischief is done. The change has come. Caste has been established, with all its attendant evils. The community, once so simple and homogeneous, is now divided into two classes, one of which looks down on the other. More cottages are built, with trim lawns and private lawn-tennis grounds, with "shandy-gaff" and "tennis-cup" concealed on tables in tents. Then the dog-cart with the groom in buckskin and boots, the Irish red setter, the saddle-horse with the banged tail, the phaeton with the two ponies, the young men in knickerbockers carrying imported racquets, the girls with the banged hair, the club, ostensibly for newspaper reading, but really for secret gin-fizzes and soda-cocktails, make their appearance, with numerous other monarchical excrescences. The original farmer, whose pristine board was the beginning of all this, has probably by this time sold enough land to the cottagers to enable him to give up taking boarders and keeping a hotel, and is able to stay in bed like a gentleman most of the winter, and sit on a bench in his shirt-sleeves all summer.

Very soon the boarder, unable to put up with the growing haughtiness of the cottager, and with exclusion from his entertainments, withdraws silently and unobtrusively from the scenes he once enjoyed so much, to seek out another unsophisticated farmer, and begin once more, probably when well on in life, with hope and strength abated, the heavy work of opening up another watering-place and developing its resources. The silent suffering there is in this process, which may be witnessed to-day in hundreds of the most beautiful spots in America, probably none know but those who have gone through it. In fact, the dislodgment along our coast and in our mountains of the boarder by the cottager is to-day the great summer tragedy of American life. Winter has tragedies of its own, which may be worse; but summer has nothing like it, nothing which imposes such a strain on character and so severely tests early training. The worst of it--the pity of it, we might say--is that this is not the expulsion of the inferior by the superior race, which is going on in so many parts of the world, and which Darwin is teaching us to look upon with equanimity. The boarder is often, if not generally, the cottager's superior in culture, in acquirements, and in variety of social experience. He does not board because he likes the food, but simply because it enables him to live in the midst of beautiful scenery. He eats the farmer's poor fare contentedly, because he finds it is sufficient to maintain his sense of natural beauty and the clearness of all his moral perceptions unimpaired, and to brace his nerves for the great battle with evil which he has been carrying on in the city, and to which he means to return after a fortnight or a month or six weeks, as the case may be. We fear, in fact, that very few indeed of our summer cottages contain half so much noble endeavor and power of self-sacrifice as the boarding-houses they are displacing.

The progress made by the cottager in driving the boarder away from some of the most attractive places, both in the hills and on the seaboard, is very steady. Among these Bar Harbor occupies a leading position. It was, for fully fifteen years after its discovery, frequented exclusively by a very high order of boarders, and probably has been the scene of more plain living and high thinking than any other summer spot on the seacoast. It was, in fact, remarkable at one time for an almost unhealthy intellectual stimulation through an exclusively fish diet. But the purity of the air and the grandeur of the scenery brought a yearly increasing tide of visitors from about 1860 onward. These visitors were, until about five years ago, almost exclusively boarders, and the development of the place as a summer resort was prodigious. The little houses of the original half farmers, half fishermen, who welcomed, or rather did not welcome, the first explorers, grew rapidly into little boarding-houses, then into big boarding-houses, then into hotels with registers. Then the hotels grew larger and larger, and the callings of the steamer more frequent, until the place became famous and crowded.

All this while, however, the hold of the boarder on it remained unshaken. He was monarch of all he surveyed. No one on the island, except the landlords, held his head higher. There was one distinction between boarders, but it was not one to wound anybody's self-love: some were "mealers," or persons eating in the hotel where they lodged; and others were "haul-mealers," or persons who were collected and brought to their food in wagons. But this classification produced no heart-burning. The mealer loved and respected the haul-mealer, or wished him in Jericho, and the haul-mealer in like manner the mealer, on general grounds, like other persons with whom he came in contact, without any reference to his place of abode. All were covered by the grand old name of boarder, and that was enough. A happier, easier, freer, and more curiously dressed summer community than Bar Harbor in those early days was not to be found on our coast.

We do not know exactly when the cottager first made his appearance on those rugged shores, but it is certain that his approaches were more insidious than they have ever been anywhere. He did not proclaim himself all at once. The first cottages were very plain structures, which he cunningly spoke of as "shanties," or "log huts," in which he simply lodged, and went to the hotels or neighboring farm-houses for his food in the simple and unpretending character of a haul-mealer. For a good while, therefore, he excited neither suspicion nor alarm, and the hotel-keepers welcomed him heartily, and all went on smoothly. Gradually, however, he threw off all disguise, bought land at high prices, and began unblushingly to erect "marine villas" on it, with everything that the name implies. He has now got possession of all the desirable sites from the Ovens down to the Great Head, and has surrounded himself with all the luxuries, just as at Newport. The consequence is, although the sea and sky and the mountains and the rocks retain all their charm, the boarder is no longer happy. He finds himself relegated to a secondary position. He is abashed when on foot or in his humble buckboard he meets the haughty cottager in his dog-cart or victoria. He has neither dog nor horse, while the cottager has both. He was once proud of staying at Rodick's or Lyman's; now he begins to be ashamed of it. He finds that the cottagers, who are the permanent residents, have a society of their own, in which he is either not welcome or is a mere outsider. He finds that the very name of boarder, which he once wore like a lily, has become a term of inferiority. Worse than all, he finds himself confounded with a still lower class, known at Bar Harbor as "the tourist"--elsewhere called the excursionist--who comes by the hundred on the steamers in linen dusters, and is compelled by force of circumstances to "do" Mount Desert in twenty-four hours, and therefore enters on his task without shame or scruple, roams over the cottager's lawn, stares into his windows, breaks his fences, and sometimes asks him for a free lunch. The boarder, of course, looks down on this man, but when both are on the road or on the piazza of the hotel how are they to be distinguished? They are not, and cannot be.

The worst of it all is, however, that the boarder finds that the cottager has enclosed some of his favorite walks. He can no longer get to them without trespassing or intruding. He can only look wistfully from the dusty high-road at the spots on which he probably once "rocked" with the girl who is now his wife, or chopped logic with professional or clerical friends, whom "the growth of the place" has long ago driven to fresh fields and pastures new. There is something very interesting and touching about these old Mount Deserters of the first period, between 1860 and 1870, who fled even before the enlargement of the hotels, and to whom cottages at Bar Harbor are almost unthinkable. One finds them in undeveloped summer resorts in out-of-the-way places along the American coast, often on the Alps or in Norway, or on the Scotch lakes, still tender, and simple, and unassuming, and cheery, older of course and generally stouter, but with the memories of the mountains, and the rocks, and the islands, of the poor food, "which made no difference, because the air was fine," still as fresh as ever, but without a particle of bitterness. They wander much, but wander as they may they find no summer resorts which can have for them the charm of Frenchman's Bay or Newport Mountain, and no vehicle which touches so many chords in their hearts as the primeval buckboard, in the days when it could only be hired as a great favor.

The cottager, too, sets no bounds to his pretensions as to territory. His policy, apparently the old policy of the conqueror everywhere, is to let the boarder go up the coast and discover the most attractive resorts, and allow him to report on them in the newspapers, write poetry about them, lay the scene of novels and plays in them, and then pursue him and eradicate him from the soil as a burden if not a nuisance. That he makes a resort far more beautiful to the eye than the boarder there is no denying. He covers it with beautiful houses; he converts the scraggy, yellow pastures into smooth, green lawns; he fills the rock crevices with flowers; he introduces better food and neater clothing and the latest dodges in plumbing. But these things are only for the few--in fact, the very few. An area which supports a hundred happy boarders will only bring one cottager to perfection. Moreover, it is impossible, no matter how much the country may flourish, that all Americans who leave the city in summer should by any effort become cottagers. The mass of them must always be boarders and remain boarders, and we would warn the cottagers that it may become dangerous to push them too hard and too far. Much farther east or north on the coast they will not go without turning on their persecutors. They will not put up with the shores of Labrador or Greenland, no matter how hot the season may be. The survival of the fittest is a great law, and has worked wonders in the animal world, but it must be remembered that it has to work in our day in subordination to that greater law of morality which makes weakness itself a strong tower of defence.

The future at all our leading seashore places, in truth, belongs to the Cottager, and it is really useless to resist him. His march along the American coast is nearly as resistless as that of the hordes who issued from the plains of Scythia to overthrow the Roman Empire. He moves on all the "choice sites" without haste, with the calm and remorselessness of the man who knows that the morrow is his. He has two tremendous forces at his back, against which no boarder can stand up. One is the growing passion, or fashion, if any one likes to call it so, of Americans to live in their own houses, both summer and winter. This is rapidly taking possession of all classes, from the New England mechanic, who puts up his shanty or tent on the seashore, to the millionaire who builds his hundred-thousand dollar villa on his thirty-thousand dollar lot. Everybody who can seeks to be at home all the year round, let the home be never so small or humble, and the life in it never so rough. This is a change in the national manners which nobody can regret, but it is a change from which the boarder must suffer, and which must cost him much wandering and many tears. The other is the spread of the love of the seashore among the vast population of the Mississippi Valley, whose wealth is becoming great, for whom long railroad journeys have no terrors, and who are likely now to send their thousands every year to compete with the "money kings" of the East for the best villa sites along the coast. And be it remembered that although our population doubles every twenty-five years, our rocky Atlantic shore, which is what all most love to seek--the sand is tame and dreary in comparison--remains a fixed quantity. It only extends from New York to Eastport, Me., and it only contains a limited number of building lots. These are now being rapidly bought up and built on, or hold on speculation, and in some places, where land only brought ten dollars an acre fifteen years ago, are held at monstrous prices.

To fight against these tendencies is useless. The wise boarder will not so do, nor waste his time in bewailing his fate. It is absurd for him to expect that long stretches of delightful shore will be left wild and uninhabited and unimproved, for him to walk over for three or four weeks every summer. Not even the Henry George regime would oust the cottager, for under it he would simply rent what he owns; a cottager he would still remain. Finally, the boarder must remember that though the cottager, like woman, when he is bad is very bad, when good is delightful. Nothing the American summer has to show can surpass a cottager, and we rejoice to know that the number of good cottagers every year grows larger. At his best though he may be stern in the assertion of his rights of property, there is no simpler, honester gentleman than he, and the moral earnestness with the want of which the more austere boarder has been apt to reproach him, grows very rapidly after he gets his lawn made and his place in order.

SUMMER REST

The question has occurred to a good many, and has been more than once publicly asked, When do the people who frequent "Summer Schools" of philosophy, theology, and the like, which are now showing themselves at some of the watering-places, get their rest or vacation? At these schools both the lecturers or "paper" readers and the audience are engaged in the same or nearly the same work as during the rest of the year, and therefore in summer get no rest. We have been asked, for instance, whether a clergyman or professor who has a period of leisure allotted to him in summer, in order that he may "recruit," as it is called, is not guilty of some sort of abuse of confidence, if, instead of amusing himself or lying fallow, he goes to a Summer School, and passes several weeks in discussions which, to be profitable either to himself or his hearers, must put some degree of strain on his faculties.

The answer undoubtedly is, that nobody goes to a Summer School who could get refreshment through sheer idleness. One of the greatest mistakes of the Middle Ages, and one which has come down to our own time in education, in theology, and in medicine, was that all men's needs, both spiritual, mental, and physical, are the same; and it long made the world a dreadful place for the exceptional or peculiar. In most things we have given up the theory. It was soonest given up as regards food, because the evidence against it was there plainest and most overwhelming, in the severe suffering inflicted on some people by things "disagreeing with them," as it was called, which others relished and profited by. It has only been surrendered with regard to children and youths, however, after a hard struggle. The idea of a young person being entitled to special treatment of any kind--that is, having in any respect a marked individuality--remains to this day odious to a great many of our theologians and teachers. It is, however, rapidly making its way, and has already obtained a secure footing in some of the colleges. It is the hotels, perhaps, which are now the strongholds of the old doctrine, and in which a person who wants what nobody else wants is considered most odious; partly, of course, because he gives extra trouble, but mainly because he is considered to be given up to a delusion about himself and his constitution. There is probably nothing which excites the anger and contempt of a summer-hotel clerk more than a request for something which is not supplied to everybody or which nobody else asks for. We remember once irritating a White Mountain hotel-keeper extremely by asking to be allowed to ride up Mount Washington alone, instead of in a party of forty. He not only refused our request, but he punished us for making it by selecting for our use the worst pony in his stable, and watching us mounting it with a diabolical sneer.

There is, however, still a good deal of intolerance about people's mode of spending their vacation. Those who take it by simply sitting still or lounging with no particular occupation, are more or less worried by the people who take their rest actively and with much movement and bustle. So also the young man who goes off fishing and hunting, on the other hand, scorns the young man who hangs about the hotels and plays lawn-tennis, or goes to picnics with the girls--a rapidly diminishing class, let us add. A correspondent, who takes a low view of sermons, wrote to us the other day complaining of some mention which recently appeared in our columns of Mount Desert as a good place for "tired clergymen," and wished to know what there was to tire them, seeing that they did nothing but produce two essays a week, which need not be very original. The truth is, however, that everybody's occupation, including that of the young man who does nothing at all, does a great deal to tire him. What probably tires a minister most is not the sermons, but his parishioners; and we suspect that nine-tenths of the ministers, if they made a clean breast of it, would confess that rest to them meant getting away from their parishioners, and not in getting away from the sermons. Sermon-writing in our day, when the area over which a preacher may select his subject is so greatly widened, is probably to a reflective man a great help and relief, as furnishing what nearly every student needs to stimulate study--a means of expression. Sustained solitary thinking is something of which very few men are capable. To keep up what is called active-mindedness nearly everyone needs somebody to talk to. Conversation with a friend is enough for most, but those who have more to say find a sermon or a magazine article just the kind of intellectual stimulus they need. What probably most wears on a clergyman's nerves are his pastoral duties, which do not consist simply in consoling people in great trials, but in listening to their fussy accounts of small ones. Nine-tenths of a minister's patients, like a doctor's, do not know what is the matter with them, and consult a physician largely because they take comfort in talking to anybody about themselves, and doctors and clergymen are the only persons who are bound to listen to them. A professor or teacher is somewhat similarly situated. His business is the most wearing of human occupations--that of putting knowledge into heads only half willing to receive it, and persuading a large number of people to do their duty to whom duty is odious.

To these men, a Summer School of philosophy or theology, or anything else, must be repose of the best sort. It gives light work of the kind they love, free from all nagging, and in good air and fine scenery. At such schools, too, one finds uses for "papers" that no periodical will print, and which no audience would assemble to listen to in a city in the busy part of the year, and to many men an audience of any sort, interested or uninterested, is a great luxury.

The persons who perhaps find it hardest to get rest in summer are brokers. Their activity in their business and the excitement attending it are so great, that quiet to them, more than to most other men, is a hell; so that their vacation is a problem not easy of solution, except to the rich ones, who have yachts and horses without limit. Even to those, every day of a vacation has to be full of movement and change. An hour not filled by some sort of activity, spent on a piazza or under a tree, is to them an hour wasted. A land where it was always afternoon would be to them the most "odious section of country" on earth. The story of one of them, who in Rome lost flesh through pining for "the corner of Wall and William," is well known. Such a man finds nearly all summer resorts vanity and vexation of spirit, because none of them provides excitement. The class known as financiers, such as presidents of banks and insurance companies, is much better off, because it has Saratoga. Its members have generally reached the time of life when men love to sit still, and when the liver is torpid, and they are generally men of means, and wear black broadcloth at all seasons, as being what they have from their youth considered outward and visible signs of "respectability" in the financial sense. What they need is a place where they can have their livers roused without exercise, and this the mineral water does for them; where they can see a good deal going on and many evidences of wealth, without moving from their chairs; and where their financial standing will follow them; and for this there is perhaps no place in the country like Saratoga. Newport has not nearly as much solidity. It is brighter and gayer and more select, but though it contains enormous fortunes, a great fortune does not here do so much for a man. It has to bear the competition of youth and beauty and polo and lawn-tennis. The young man with little besides a polo pony, an imported racquet, and good looks counts for a good deal at Newport; at Saratoga he would be nobody.

THE SURVIVAL OF TYPES

The London **Daily News**, in the course of an article on what it calls "International Reproaches," refers to the fact that there is much that is "traditional" in them. It thinks that, both in America and in France, the qualities and peculiarities attributed to English people are derived, to a great extent, less from experience than from inherited tradition. "We hear that Englishmen are rude to ladies; that they fail to yield them precedence at the ticket-offices of steamboats and railway stations; that they complain of everything that is given them as food; that they occupy more than their share of public conveyances with multitudinous wraps, sticks, and umbrellas. They assert themselves, it would seem, when they have placed 3,000 miles between themselves and their old home. There is, however, in all these complaints the ring of old coin." In the same way it says that the Parisian of the boulevards still believes the English man to be a creature who wears long red whiskers of the mutton-chop species, and wears a plaid--although, as a matter of fact, the typical Englishman of to-day does not look like this at all.

Anyone interested in the matter might make a very queer collection of types which, having disappeared from actual life, survive in the popular imagination, and by surviving keep alive international prejudice, hostility, suspicion, or distrust, and which go on doing duty in this way for years and years, until suddenly some fine day it is discovered that they are out of date and must in future be dispensed with.

There is, for instance, our old friend, the stage Irishman. How often have our hearts been touched by the qualities of gratitude, devotion to sentiment, faithful friendship, and heroism of this noble creature. No doubt, there must have been a time when he was as common in Ireland as he has been in our day in melodrama. But the Irishman, as he exists in New York, and as he is described by those who have seen him at home, is strangely unlike the type. He is a decidedly practical, hard-headed man, with a keen eye to the main chance, a considerable fondness for fighting, and a disposition which we should call the reverse of sentimental. Harrigan and Hart represent the actual Irishman in America capitally at their little theatre in Broadway, yet the stage Irishman is to multitudes of Americans a more real creature than the actual Irishman, and we suppose there is hardly a Democratic statesman from one end of the country to the other who has not constantly before his mind an image of him, by the contemplation of which he solves many of the knottiest problems of contemporary politics.

Then there is the Dundreary Englishman, first-cousin or lineal descendant of the Englishman so dear to the French imagination. Dundreary really represents, as we know very well, when we think about it, a past type of swell as extinct as the dodo. It is not common any longer for English swells to change all their rs to ws, and to spice their sentences with "aw-aws." We have numbers of them over here every year, but we do not hear them talk nowadays the once familiar Dundreary language. Yet there is hardly a newspaper in the United States whose funny man does not assume for the benefit of his readers that Dundreary is alive, and every now and then reproduce him with gusto. It is not in *Punch* that we find Dundreary, but in the funny department of the Oshkosh *Monitor* and the "All Sorts" column of the Bungtown *Clarion*. Even *Puck* contributes to perpetuate the belief in the continued existence of Dundreary by devoting a column a week to observations on American society in the Dundreary dialect, which thirty years ago might have been decidedly funny.

Punch still has John Bull as a national type; but it shows great reserve in the use of him, and now continually resorts to Britannia as a substitute. Is not this because our old friend John is now only a survival, a tradition of the past? The bluff, stout, honest, red-faced, irascible rural person--of whom the photographs of John Bright remind us--has really been supplanted by a more modern, thinner, nervous, intellectual, astute type. For English use the Yankee type of Uncle Sam still seems to represent America, although it belongs to the past as much as slavery or the stage-coach. He would be a bold man who should undertake to say what the national type is now; but it is safe to say that it is not a long, thin, cute Yankee, dressed in a swallow-tailed coat with brass buttons, whittling a stick, and interlarding his conversation with "I swan!" and "I calc'late." If Mr. Lowell were writing the "Biglow Papers" now, would "Uncle S." serve his purpose as he did during the war? By a merciful dispensation of Providence, however, Brother Jonathan and Uncle Sam still live on in the imaginations of large masses of conservative Englishmen, and no doubt enable many a Tory to people the United States with a race as alien from that which actually inhabits it as Zulus would be.

In the same way it may be possible--to the Providence that guides the destinies of nations nothing is impossible--that the rude Englishman is, as the **Daily News** suggests, getting to be a survival. The **Daily News's** portrait of him is fair enough, though it would require Americans who have suffered from him to do him real justice. He is, or, was, a very rude person, and always seemed to take great delight in "asserting himself" in such a way as to produce as much general annoyance and discomfort as possible. During the war he had a brilliant career. He used to come over and express great surprise at the silly fuss made about the Constitution and secession, and profess an entire inability to discover what it was "all about." If they want to go, he always said, why don't you let 'em go? What is the use of fighting about the meaning of a word in the dictionary? It was in small things as in great. When he went into society he dressed to suit himself, and not as gentlemen in England or anywhere else do, thus contriving to exhibit a general contempt for his host and his friends. When his meek entertainer ventured to offer him some American dish which he did not like, he would frankly warn his companions against it; and if he asked for sugar in his coffee he would, in the same outspoken way, explain that he always sweetened it "when it was bad." One of his favorite topics of conversation was the awful corruption and rottenness of American society and politics, and he dwelt so much upon this that it often seemed as if what he was really interested in was to find out whether the people he was staying with, and being entertained by, were not themselves, if the truth were known, rotten to the core.

He was a very rude man, and he did exist. But is he gone, or going? Is the time coming when we shall have to regard him too as a survival, and admit that the rude Englishman is a creature of the past? Time and continued international experience can alone settle this question. There are, however, bitter memories of past sufferings at his hands in hundreds of American homes, that make it better for both countries not to probe the subject too deeply.

WILL WIMBLES

Mr. Thomas Hughes's attempt to provide a refuge in Tennessee for the large class of young Englishmen whom he calls "Will Wimbles," after one of Sir Roger de Coverley's friends in Addison's *Spectator*, is said to be a failure, owing mainly to the poverty of the land and the remoteness of the markets. An acute writer in the *Pall Mall Gazette* maintains that there is another and more potent cause to be found in the quality of the Will Wimbles. The Will Wimbles are the young men who are educated in the public schools and universities, or at least in the public schools, and are turned out into the world between eighteen and twenty-one, without any special training whatever, but with the manners and instincts of gentlemen, and with entire willingness to take to any calling but the lower walks of "trade." The great body of them are the sons of middle-class parents--clergymen, doctors, lawyers, and small squires--whose means are very moderate, and who have to submit to more or less privation in order to send their sons to the public schools at all. They do it in order to launch them in the world unmistakably in the gentle class, and in order to enable them to form their first social relations in that class. Unfortunately, however, as the writer in the *Pall Mall Gazette* points out, the tone and temper of the public schools, and their way of looking at life, are the products of a vague, but none the less powerful, assumption that every boy is the son of a man with about five thousand pounds a year. The whole atmosphere of the school is permeated with this assumption. The boys' code of manners is formed in it. Their intercourse with each other is more or less influenced by it, and they all look out on the world, up to their last day at school, with the eyes of youths whose home is a well-equipped manor-house surrounded by a prosperous estate.

The love of the middle-class Englishman of every age for this point of view is curiously exemplified in the social articles, not only in the "society paper," properly so called, but in the **Saturday Review**. The troubles and perplexities and minor disappointments of life form a favorite topic with the writer of the "sub-leaders" in this last-named paper, but they are always of the troubles, perplexities, and disappointments of a landed gentleman who keeps hunters, and has a stud groom and extensive covers. He hardly ever examines the state of mind of anyone less well-to-do than a younger son whose means only allow him to hunt two days in a week instead of six, and who has to rely on invitations for his shooting. These and their sisters, cousins, and aunts, apparently form the reviewer's entire world, and the only world in which there are any social phenomena worth discussion. It is, in other words, a world made up exclusively of "gentlemen," and of the persons, male and female, who wait upon them. Its sorrows are the sorrows of gentlemen, and arise mostly out of the failure of some amusement, or the loss of the money with which amusements are provided, the missing of some social distinction, or the misconduct of "upper servants." It is, however, really the only world that the English public-school boy or university man sees, or hears of, or thinks about while in **statu pupillari**. This is true, let his own home be never so modest, or the sacrifices made by his father to secure him the fashionable curriculum be never so painful. The result is, of course, that when his "education" is finished, he is really only prepared for what is technically called a gentleman's life. He has only thought of certain employments as possible to him, and all these are exceedingly hard to get. The manners of the great bulk of mankind, too, are more or less repulsive to him, and so is a good deal of the popular morality. In short, he is turned out a Will Wimble--or, in other words, a good-hearted, kindly, gentlemanly, honorable fellow, who is, however, entirely unfitted for the social **milieu**, in which he must not only live, but make a living.

Mr. Hughes's idea has been that, though he dislikes trade, and is a little too nice for it as now carried on, at least on the retail side, he has an innate liking and readiness for agriculture, and that, if enabled to till the soil under pleasant, or at least not too novel, social conditions, he would do it successfully. Out of this the Rugby, Tenn., experiment has grown, and if it has not actually failed, as some say, it is certainly too early to pronounce it a success. At all events, the signs that it is going to fail are numerous. Among them is the deep disappointment of the settlers, few of whom probably realized not only the monotony and drudgery of labor in the fields--these things can be borne by men with stout hearts and strong arms--but its effect in unfitting a man for any kind of amusement. There has been much delusion on this subject in this country, where far more is known by the reading class about all kinds of manual labor than is known in England. The possibility of working hard in the fields and keeping up at the same time some process of intellectual culture, has been much preached among us both by educational projectors and social reformers, though nearly every man who listens to them here knows the effect of physical toil in the open air in producing sleepiness and mental inertness. It is not surprising, therefore, that it should find ready acceptance in England among people who think ability to bear a hard day on the moors after grouse, or a long run in the saddle after the hounds, argues capacity to hoe potatoes or corn for twelve hours, and settle down in the evening, after a bath and a good dinner, to Dante, or Wallace, or Huxley.

Will Wimbles are much less common among us than in England. We fortunately have not a dozen great endowments used in turning them out, or a large and rich society occupied in spreading the gentlemanly view of life. But they, nevertheless, are more numerous than is altogether pleasant. The difficulty which our college graduate experiences in getting room for what the newspapers call his "bark" on the stream of life, is one of the standing jokes of our light literature. We have no schools which take the place of the English public schools in our scheme of education. But the view of life which prevails in the English public schools and turns out the Will Wimbles, is more or less prevalent in our colleges, and tends to spread as the wealth of the class which sends its boys to college increases. In other words, colleges are to a much greater extent than they used to be places in which social relations are found, rather than places of preparation for the active work of life. This last character, indeed, they almost wholly lost when they ceased to have the training of ministers as their main function. Scarcely any man who can afford it now likes to refuse his son a college education if the boy wants it; but probably not one boy in one thousand can say, five years after graduating, that he has been helped by his college education in making his start in life. It may have been never so useful to him as a means of moral and intellectual culture, but it has not helped to adapt him to the environment in which he has to live and work; or, in other words, to a world in which not one man in a thousand has either the manners or cultivation of a gentleman, or changes his shirt more than once a week, or eats with a fork.

College education is prevented from suffering as much from this source in popular estimation in England as it does here, by the fact that, owing to the peculiar political traditions of the country, college-bred men begin life in a large number of cases in possession of great advantages of other kinds, such as hereditary wealth. Here they have almost all to face the world on their own merits, and in so far as they face it feebly or unskilfully their defects are set down in the popular mind to the fact that they went to college. If the discredit ended here, it would perhaps be of small consequence. But it may be safely said that the college graduate is never seen groping about in a helpless and timid way for "a position," and shrinking from the turmoil and dirt of some walks of life, without spreading among the uncultivated a contempt for culture and increasing their confidence in the rule of thumb. The mere "going to college" is recognized as a sign of pecuniary ease, and of a desire for social advancement, but not as preparation for the kind of work which the bulk of the community is doing, and thus makes mental culture seem less desirable, and cultivated men less potent, especially in politics.

The question is a serious one for all colleges, and it is not here only, but in England and France, that it is undergoing grave consideration. In Germany society may be said to have been organized as an appendage to the universities, but here the universities are simply appendages to society, which is continually doubting whether their existence can be justified.

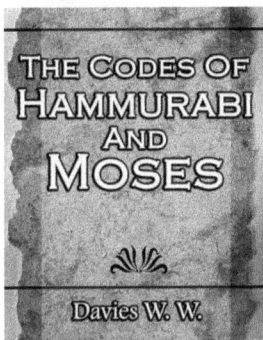

The Codes Of Hammurabi And Moses
W. W. Davies

QTY

The discovery of the Hammurabi Code is one of the greatest achievements of archaeology, and is of paramount interest, not only to the student of the Bible, but also to all those interested in ancient history...

Religion   ISBN: *1-59462-338-4*   Pages:132
MSRP $12.95

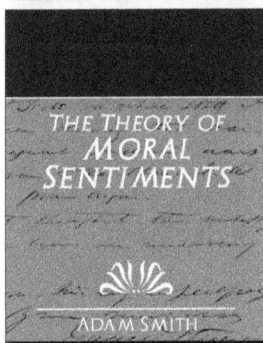

The Theory of Moral Sentiments
Adam Smith

QTY

This work from 1749. contains original theories of conscience amd moral judgment and it is the foundation for systemof morals.

Philosophy ISBN: *1-59462-777-0*   Pages:536
MSRP $19.95

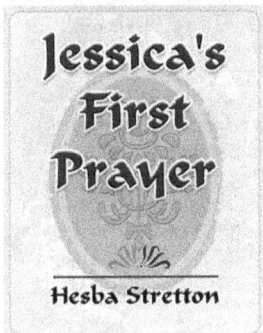

Jessica's First Prayer
Hesba Stretton

QTY

In a screened and secluded corner of one of the many railway-bridges which span the streets of London there could be seen a few years ago, from five o'clock every morning until half past eight, a tidily set-out coffee-stall, consisting of a trestle and board, upon which stood two large tin cans, with a small fire of charcoal burning under each so as to keep the coffee boiling during the early hours of the morning when the work-people were thronging into the city on their way to their daily toil...

Childrens   ISBN: *1-59462-373-2*   Pages:84
MSRP $9.95

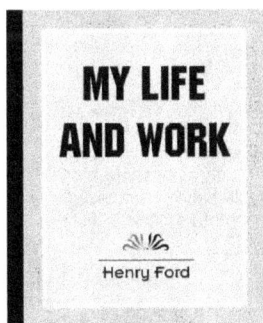

My Life and Work
Henry Ford

QTY

Henry Ford revolutionized the world with his implementation of mass production for the Model T automobile. Gain valuable business insight into his life and work with his own auto-biography... "We have only started on our development of our country we have not as yet, with all our talk of wonderful progress, done more than scratch the surface. The progress has been wonderful enough but..."

Biographies/ ISBN: *1-59462-198-5*   Pages:300
MSRP $21.95

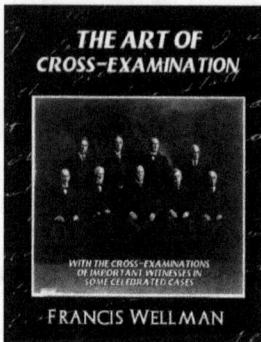

The Art of Cross-Examination
Francis Wellman

QTY

I presume it is the experience of every author, after his first book is published upon an important subject, to be almost overwhelmed with a wealth of ideas and illustrations which could readily have been included in his book, and which to his own mind, at least, seem to make a second edition inevitable. Such certainly was the case with me; and when the first edition had reached its sixth impression in five months, I rejoiced to learn that it seemed to my publishers that the book had met with a sufficiently favorable reception to justify a second and considerably enlarged edition. ..

Pages:412

Reference   ISBN: *1-59462-647-2*   *MSRP $19.95*

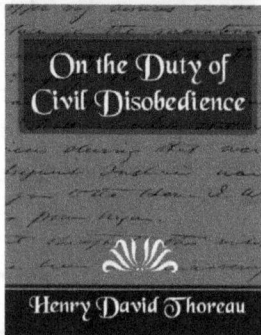

On the Duty of Civil Disobedience
Henry David Thoreau

QTY

Thoreau wrote his famous essay, On the Duty of Civil Disobedience, as a protest against an unjust but popular war and the immoral but popular institution of slave-owning. He did more than write—he declined to pay his taxes, and was hauled off to gaol in consequence. Who can say how much this refusal of his hastened the end of the war and of slavery ?

Law   ISBN: *1-59462-747-9*   **Pages:48**

MSRP $7.45

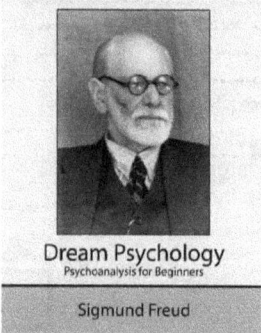

Dream Psychology Psychoanalysis for Beginners
Sigmund Freud

QTY

Sigmund Freud, born Sigismund Schlomo Freud (May 6, 1856 - September 23, 1939), was a Jewish-Austrian neurologist and psychiatrist who co-founded the psychoanalytic school of psychology. Freud is best known for his theories of the unconscious mind, especially involving the mechanism of repression; his redefinition of sexual desire as mobile and directed towards a wide variety of objects; and his therapeutic techniques, especially his understanding of transference in the therapeutic relationship and the presumed value of dreams as sources of insight into unconscious desires.

Pages:196

Psychology   ISBN: *1-59462-905-6*   *MSRP $15.45*

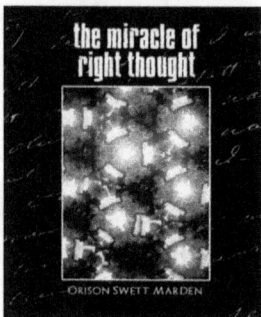

The Miracle of Right Thought
Orison Swett Marden

QTY

Believe with all of your heart that you will do what you were made to do. When the mind has once formed the habit of holding cheerful, happy, prosperous pictures, it will not be easy to form the opposite habit. It does not matter how improbable or how far away this realization may see, or how dark the prospects may be, if we visualize them as best we can, as vividly as possible, hold tenaciously to them and vigorously struggle to attain them, they will gradually become actualized, realized in the life. But a desire, a longing without endeavor, a yearning abandoned or held indifferently will vanish without realization.

Pages:360

Self Help   ISBN: *1-59462-644-8*   *MSRP $25.45*

QTY

The Rosicrucian Cosmo-Conception Mystic Christianity *by Max Heindel*   ISBN: *1-59462-188-8* **$38.95**
The Rosicrucian Cosmo-conception is not dogmatic, neither does it appeal to any other authority than the reason of the student. It is: not controversial, but is: sent forth in the, hope that it may help to clear...   New Age/Religion Pages 646

Abandonment To Divine Providence *by Jean-Pierre de Caussade*   ISBN: *1-59462-228-0* **$25.95**
"The Rev. Jean Pierre de Caussade was one of the most remarkable spiritual writers of the Society of Jesus in France in the 18th Century. His death took place at Toulouse in 1751. His works have gone through many editions and have been republished...   Inspirational/Religion Pages 400

Mental Chemistry *by Charles Haanel*   ISBN: *1-59462-192-6* **$23.95**
Mental Chemistry allows the change of material conditions by combining and appropriately utilizing the power of the mind. Much like applied chemistry creates something new and unique out of careful combinations of chemicals the mastery of mental chemistry...   New Age Pages 354

The Letters of Robert Browning and Elizabeth Barret Barrett 1845-1846 vol II   ISBN: *1-59462-193-4* **$35.95**
by Robert Browning and Elizabeth Barrett   Biographies Pages 596

Gleanings In Genesis (volume I) *by Arthur W. Pink*   ISBN: *1-59462-130-6* **$27.45**
Appropriately has Genesis been termed "the seed plot of the Bible" for in it we have, in germ form, almost all of the great doctrines which are afterwards fully developed in the books of Scripture which follow...   Religion/Inspirational Pages 420

The Master Key *by L. W. de Laurence*   ISBN: *1-59462-001-6* **$30.95**
In no branch of human knowledge has there been a more lively increase of the spirit of research during the past few years than in the study of Psychology, Concentration and Mental Discipline. The requests for authentic lessons in Thought Control, Mental Discipline and...   New Age/Business Pages 422

The Lesser Key Of Solomon Goetia *by L. W. de Laurence*   ISBN: *1-59462-092-X* **$9.95**
This translation of the first book of the "Lernegton" which is now for the first time made accessible to students of Talismanic Magic was done, after careful collation and edition, from numerous Ancient Manuscripts in Hebrew, Latin, and French...   New Age/Occult Pages 92

Rubaiyat Of Omar Khayyam *by Edward Fitzgerald*   ISBN:*1-59462-332-5* **$13.95**
Edward Fitzgerald, whom the world has already learned, in spite of his own efforts to remain within the shadow of anonymity, to look upon as one of the rarest poets of the century, was born at Bredfield, in Suffolk, on the 31st of March, 1809. He was the third son of John Purcell...   Music Pages 172

Ancient Law *by Henry Maine*   ISBN: *1-59462-128-4* **$29.95**
The chief object of the following pages is to indicate some of the earliest ideas of mankind, as they are reflected in Ancient Law, and to point out the relation of those ideas to modern thought.   Religion/History Pages 452

Far-Away Stories *by William J. Locke*   ISBN: *1-59462-129-2* **$19.45**
"Good wine needs no bush, but a collection of mixed vintages does. And this book is just such a collection. Some of the stories I do not want to remain buried for ever in the museum files of dead magazine-numbers an author's not unpardonable vanity..."   Fiction Pages 272

Life of David Crockett *by David Crockett*   ISBN: *1-59462-250-7* **$27.45**
"Colonel David Crockett was one of the most remarkable men of the times in which he lived. Born in humble life, but gifted with a strong will, an indomitable courage, and unremitting perseverance...   Biographies/New Age Pages 424

Lip-Reading *by Edward Nitchie*   ISBN: *1-59462-206-X* **$25.95**
Edward B. Nitchie, founder of the New York School for the Hard of Hearing, now the Nitchie School of Lip-Reading, Inc, wrote "LIP-READING Principles and Practice". The development and perfecting of this meritorious work on lip-reading was an undertaking...   How-to Pages 400

A Handbook of Suggestive Therapeutics, Applied Hypnotism, Psychic Science   ISBN: *1-59462-214-0* **$24.95**
by Henry Munro   Health/New Age/Health/Self-help Pages 376

A Doll's House: and Two Other Plays *by Henrik Ibsen*   ISBN: *1-59462-112-8* **$19.95**
Henrik Ibsen created this classic when in revolutionary 1848 Rome. Introducing some striking concepts in playwriting for the realist genre, this play has been studied the world over.   Fiction/Classics/Plays 308

The Light of Asia *by sir Edwin Arnold*   ISBN: *1-59462-204-3* **$13.95**
In this poetic masterpiece, Edwin Arnold describes the life and teachings of Buddha. The man who was to become known as Buddha to the world was born as Prince Gautama of India but he rejected the worldly riches and abandoned the reigns of power when...   Religion/History/Biographies Pages 170

The Complete Works of Guy de Maupassant *by Guy de Maupassant*   ISBN: *1-59462-157-8* **$16.95**
"For days and days, nights and nights, I had dreamed of that first kiss which was to consecrate our engagement, and I knew not on what spot I should put my lips..."   Fiction/Classics Pages 240

The Art of Cross-Examination *by Francis L. Wellman*   ISBN: *1-59462-309-0* **$26.95**
Written by a renowned trial lawyer, Wellman imparts his experience and uses case studies to explain how to use psychology to extract desired information through questioning.   How-to/Science/Reference Pages 408

Answered or Unanswered? *by Louisa Vaughan*   ISBN: *1-59462-248-5* **$10.95**
Miracles of Faith in China   Religion Pages 112

The Edinburgh Lectures on Mental Science (1909) *by Thomas*   ISBN: *1-59462-008-3* **$11.95**
This book contains the substance of a course of lectures recently given by the writer in the Queen Street Hail, Edinburgh. Its purpose is to indicate the Natural Principles governing the relation between Mental Action and Material Conditions...   New Age/Psychology Pages 148

Ayesha *by H. Rider Haggard*   ISBN: *1-59462-301-5* **$24.95**
Verily and indeed it is the unexpected that happens! Probably if there was one person upon the earth from whom the Editor of this, and of a certain previous history, did not expect to hear again...   Classics Pages 380

Ayala's Angel *by Anthony Trollope*   ISBN: *1-59462-352-X* **$29.95**
The two girls were both pretty, but Lucy who was twenty-one who supposed to be simple and comparatively unattractive, whereas Ayala was credited, as her Bombwhat romantic name might show, with poetic charm and a taste for romance. Ayala when her father died was nineteen...   Fiction Pages 484

The American Commonwealth *by James Bryce*   ISBN: *1-59462-286-8* **$34.45**
An interpretation of American democratic political theory. It examines political mechanics and society from the perspective of Scotsman James Bryce   Politics Pages 572

Stories of the Pilgrims *by Margaret P. Pumphrey*   ISBN: *1-59462-116-0* **$17.95**
This book explores pilgrims religious oppression in England as well as their escape to Holland and eventual crossing to America on the Mayflower, and their early days in New England...   History Pages 268

QTY

The Fasting Cure *by Sinclair Upton*   ISBN: *1-59462-222-1*   **$13.95**

In the Cosmopolitan Magazine for May, 1910, and in the Contemporary Review (London) for April, 1910, I published an article dealing with my experiences in fasting. I have written a great many magazine articles, but never one which attracted so much attention...   New Age/Self Help/Health Pages 164

Hebrew Astrology *by Sepharial*   ISBN: *1-59462-308-2*   **$13.45**

In these days of advanced thinking it is a matter of common observation that we have left many of the old landmarks behind and that we are now pressing forward to greater heights and to a wider horizon than that which represented the mind-content of our progenitors...   Astrology Pages 144

Thought Vibration or The Law of Attraction in the Thought World   ISBN: *1-59462-127-6*   **$12.95**

by William Walker Atkinson   Psychology/Religion Pages 144

Optimism *by Helen Keller*   ISBN: *1-59462-108-X*   **$15.95**

Helen Keller was blind, deaf, and mute since 19 months old, yet famously learned how to overcome these handicaps, communicate with the world, and spread her lectures promoting optimism. An inspiring read for everyone...   Biographies/Inspirational Pages 84

Sara Crewe *by Frances Burnett*   ISBN: *1-59462-360-0*   **$9.45**

In the first place, Miss Minchin lived in London. Her home was a large, dull, tall one, in a large, dull square, where all the houses were alike, and all the sparrows were alike, and where all the door-knockers made the same heavy sound...   Childrens/Classic Pages 88

The Autobiography of Benjamin Franklin *by Benjamin Franklin*   ISBN: *1-59462-135-7*   **$24.95**

The Autobiography of Benjamin Franklin has probably been more extensively read than any other American historical work, and no other book of its kind has had such ups and downs of fortune. Franklin lived for many years in England, where he was agent...   Biographies/History Pages 332

Name	
Email	
Telephone	
Address	
City, State ZIP	

☐ **Credit Card**   ☐ **Check / Money Order**

Credit Card Number	
Expiration Date	
Signature	

Please Mail to: Book Jungle
PO Box 2226
Champaign, IL 61825
or Fax to: 630-214-0564

ORDERING INFORMATION

web*: www.bookjungle.com*
email*: sales@bookjungle.com*
fax*: 630-214-0564*
mail*: Book Jungle PO Box 2226 Champaign, IL 61825*
or PayPal *to sales@bookjungle.com*

Please contact us for bulk discounts

DIRECT-ORDER TERMS

**20% Discount if You Order
Two or More Books**
Free Domestic Shipping!
Accepted: Master Card, Visa,
Discover, American Express

www.ingramcontent.com/pod-product-compliance
Lightning Source LLC
Chambersburg PA
CBHW080507110426
42742CB00017B/3026